W9-CLF-151

SOME OF THESE DAYS

by

Natalie Gaupp

Contact Information
Natalie Gaupp
7907 Bonito Drive
Arlington, TX 76002
817.437.3700
ngaupp@uta.edu

SOME OF THESE DAYS by Natalie Gaupp

Produced and performed by the Maverick Theatre Company for MAVPLAYS 2017
Presented in the University of Texas at Arlington Studio Theatre
Opening Night: April 13, 2017

The production featured the following company members (in order of appearance):
RADIO BROADCASTER 1 (voice-over): Joe Chapa
COURTENAY DEES: Bradley Atuba
YOUNG COURTENAY: Rodney Sanders
YOUNG JACK: Neil A. Farrell
EUGENIA HOLLIS: Detra Payne
LOLA RAE ALLEN: Samantha Lindberg
RADIO BROADCASTER 2 (voice-over): Tiffany Sellers
JEWEL DEES: Victoria Raines
JACK FORNETT: Stephen Wykle

UTA Department of Theatre Arts Chair and Maverick Theatre Company Producer: Kim LaFontaine
UTA Department of Theatre Arts Associate Chair: Andrew Gaupp
Director: Natalie Gaupp
Stage Manager: Megan E. Gates
Assistant Stage Manager: Tanya Garcia
Scenic Design: Michelle Harvey
Costume Design: Kris O'Brien
Lighting Design: Kat Fahrenthold
Sound Design: Jared Land
Production Manager: Jared Land
Box Office Services: Linda Panther
Publicist: Julienne Greer

The play is dedicated to Jewel Odessa Scroggins and Lola Gertrude Mercer.

SOME OF THESE DAYS by Natalie Gaupp

The Characters (in order of appearance)
RADIO BROADCASTER 1 (voice-over): A male voice with Cuban/Spanish dialect traces.
COURTENAY DEES: African-American male, mid-sixties, heavy set.
YOUNG COURTENAY: COURTENAY DEES in his mid-twenties, thin and wiry.
YOUNG JACK: JACK FORNETT in his mid-twenties, a bit brawny,
EUGENIA HOLLIS: African-American female, tremendous charisma, mid-to-late fifties.
LOLA RAE ALLEN: Anglo female, twenty, buxom and charming.
RADIO BROADCASTER 2 (voice-over): A female voice with a Mid-American dialect.
JEWEL DEES: African-American female, mid-twenties, classically beautiful, wise.
JACK FORNETT: Anglo male, mid-sixties, average build.

Notes from the Playwright
YOUNG COURTENAY and YOUNG JACK are *not* to be played by the same actors portraying the contemporary COURTENAY and JACK.

Actor-musicians are *not* crucial to the casting of any of the roles; a director may choose to creatively use pre-recorded music, to shadow the actors, or to use any innovation of his/her choice in order to establish the roles of YOUNG COURTENAY, YOUNG JACK and COURTENAY as musicians.

The various "memory" scenes of the play are *not* to be played on fully realized sets. I imagine COURTENAY's Miami Beach apartment to be the only fully realized setting of the play. The settings of the "memory" scenes should have a skeletal quality, using only the most minimal of set pieces. Sepia tone slide images as backdrops for the "memory" scenes are suggested, or any creative concept using minimalism.

"Bring me all of your dreams,
 You dreamers,
 Bring me all of your heart melodies
 That I may wrap them
 In a blue cloud-cloth
 Away from the too-rough fingers
 Of the world."

"I asked you, baby,
 If you understood—
 You told me that you didn't
 But you thought you would."

—*Langston Hughes*

SOME OF THESE DAYS

by

Natalie Gaupp

ACT I
scene i

(In black, we hear the slow, stark melody line of a Big Band standard, perhaps "Old Yazoo," played on clarinet. It begins at a hushed tone, *progressively* climbing to full volume. The feeling is moody, blue, very bittersweet. After approximately 30 seconds, the music fades and the stark ringing of a telephone is heard coupled with the hushed sound of a radio tuned to an all-news station.

Lights up as the telephone ringing/radio broadcast continues. It is late 1988. A one room, hot and cold running apartment is seen—located within an old, yet-to-be restored Art Deco District residence in Miami Beach. Although the apartment is small and needs repair, there is charm: the architecture reflects the art deco era (the room was once part of a suite in a small, full-service hotel). The apartment is furnished with found items, some interesting, some trash. The telephone ringing emits from an old trimline phone on the wall in kitchen area. Near a ragged sofa, the radio sits on a small side table.

A large trunk is in the livingroom area: it is plastered with découpage work and stickers identifying past travels, and is covered over with things that need to be thrown out—cardboard boxes, a broken lamp, newspapers, *et cetera*— and is only slightly visible. A trombone case is near the apartment door, with a thin, slightly tattered, knit cardigan tossed over it.

The living areas of the apartment—what should be the livingroom/bedroom, the kitchen, a "bathroom" hidden behind a screen/divider—are only barely discernible from one another. A small coat closet near the door serves as the only closet. A small window in the kitchen area is seen open.

On the ragged sofa—which looks like a person could fall into it and sleep a sleep of dreams--is COURTENAY DEES, mid-sixties. He is a black man, large and strong looking, with a face which holds no bitterness; handsome, but not in a striking way—more in a warm and comfortable way. He wears an old Hawaiian wedding shirt, unbuttoned, and a pair of well-worn khaki pants—this should be representative of the type of clothing he wears throughout. He is rousing from a fitful sleep.)

RADIO BROADCASTER 1
(A male voice with Cuban/Spanish dialect traces.)
…notably that Lieutenant General Colin L. Powell, President Reagan's national security advisor, has been nominated for the rank of full general and is expected to take over the Army's Forces Command in early '89.

(COURTENAY wakes and begins to sit up, shooting a hateful stare at the persistently ringing telephone.)

Moving on: NBC has won the rights for U.S. television coverage of the next series of Olympic Games.

(COURTENAY slowly stands and moves toward the phone.)

The network is expected to sell coverage to cable television to reduce the costs of its $401 million bid to broadcast the 1992 games in Barcelona.

(As COURTENAY arrives at the phone, he stares it down for a moment, then acquiesces and picks it up.)

COURTENAY
Hello. Yeah, Courtenay Dees-- you got him, you got the man. For who? You're lookin' for who? Awwww, just hang on there a second...

RADIO BROADCASTER 1
Next: Looks like South Beach is the place to be this weekend. Up next we'll have the three day forecast for Dade and Broward counties, as well as South Florida beach advisories and small craft warnings.

(COURTENAY goes to the radio and it off.)

COURTENAY
Okay now...you're speaking here to Courtenay Dees, yeah—but you say you're lookin' for one Jack Fornett? Uhm-hmm—*and you'd be?*
(Pause. When COURTENAY speaks again it is obvious he is a little taken back.)
Yeah...sure. Yeah, I see.
(Longer pause, he becomes a bit lost.)
What? I-I'm here. Go on ahead, I…
(Slowly.)

COURTENAY cont'd

I'm still here.

(Lights fade to black as COURTENAY, somewhat dazed, stares out, listening to the telephone receiver.)

(Lights up. The year is 1948. A slide projection reflects a street in downtown St. Louis; little or no set dressing complements this black and white image, acting as a backdrop. YOUNG COURTENAY, seen in his mid-twenties, has a baby face that would cause girls to swoon, and a body lean as a rail. He plays extemporaneously on his trombone; his music is lively...something reminiscent of a big band melody line crossed with raw, freeform jazz. YOUNG COURTENAY's trombone case is opened for passersby to toss in coins; the coins gleam on the sidewalk and in/on the case.

YOUNG JACK, also in his mid-twenties, looks on as YOUNG COURTENAY plays. He is a handsome young white man—but not in a mild or comfortable way—there is something "dangerous" about him and his looks. YOUNG JACK connects with YOUNG COURTENAY's music, responding with affirmation—and even laughter as YOUNG COURTENAY experiments with his music creating something of an internal dialogue within the phrases.

YOUNG COURTENAY glances occasionally—and somewhat uneasily—at YOUNG JACK. Finally, YOUNG COURTENAY begins to wind down—and then stops playing completely. He stares at YOUNG JACK.)

Y. JACK

Oh, nowwww. Don't stop on my account. You were really goin' there. That melody... the— your through line—you're workin' that out...from yesterday. Just a little more playin' around with it, and you got it.

Y. COURTENAY

You a cop or somethin'?

Y. JACK

What, me? No. Me a cop?

Y. COURTENAY

Then you gonna tell me why you been comin' around here and starin' me down?

Y. JACK

Am I causin' some kinda problem here?

Y. COURTENAY

I didn't say that. Just askin' why. Are you a talent scout?

Y. JACK

Maybe it's none of your business.

Y. COURTENAY

Maybe. But after three afternoons of you standin' there, lookin' me over, I start thinkin' things. You gonna offer me a job or take me out to the movies?

Y. JACK

(Feeling overly defensive/combative.)

You gettin' a smart mouth with me? You tryin' to be flip?

Y. COURTENAY

(Begins to pack up his trombone and case.)

I'm not tryin' anything with you. I'm not a body to cause trouble. I'm just playing for bus fare to get home. I'm not out to cause any kinda trouble.

Y. JACK

(After a beat.)

Look, look—stop. I'm not tryin' to shut ya down. I've just been...you gotta good sound. That's it. You got somethin' real. You know how to make it speak.

Y. COURTENAY

(Pauses; looks at Y. JACK.)

What? You some kinda hepcat?

Y. JACK

I play. I'm with the Tiny Stevens Orchestra. We're finishin' up a run at the Casa Loma. You play anywhere but on the street?

Y. COURTENAY

There's some guys I hook up with in the evening...couple of places over to Market Street. But I'm on my way outta here. Florida.

Y. JACK

Florida's home?

> **Y. COURTENAY**
>
Eatonville.

> **Y. JACK**
>
Never heard of it.

> **Y. COURTENAY**
>
No reason you should.

> **Y. JACK**
>
In a real big hurry to get back there?

> **Y. COURTENAY**
> (Not combatively.)
>
You ask a lotta questions.

> **Y. JACK**
>
You got a problem with questions?

> **Y. COURTENAY**
>
I don't have a problem with anything about you. I don't want any trouble.

> **Y. JACK**
>
Oh, God. Look. I haven't been waitin' around here to pick a fight with you. I'm not out to get you or nothin' like that...I just—
> (Not sure how to ask.)
>
I've been thinkin' and...

> **Y. COURTENAY**
> (In reference to the last three days.)
>
You've been thinkin' all this time?

> **Y. JACK**
>
Yeah. I...I know how you can get a gig, a pretty good one if you want it.

> **Y. COURTENAY**
>
What do you know?

> **Y. JACK**
>
But the thing is—if you're headed to Florida...

> **Y. COURTENAY**
>
There could be a change of plans—maybe.

Y. JACK

We're losin' our trombone player. He's found himself some big high dollar gig and he's not even givin' any kinda notice. He's outta here.

Y. COURTENAY

I believe St. Louis's probably got a least one trombone player that'd fit in fine with Tiny Stevens...if you know what I mean.

Y. JACK

Tiny Stevens'd be fine about you.

Y. COURTENAY

No, I don't mean to look down on your offer...I just know.

Y. JACK

If you want it, I could get you in. Period.

Y. COURTENAY

You don't think Mr. Stevens could find himself a trombone player without—

Y. JACK

He could find anybody...*your* sound is what I—what he needs.

Y. COURTENAY

He might need my sound, but does he need my black face?

Y. JACK

(After a beat.)
Oh, nowwww—if you're gonna be like that...

Y. COURTENAY

I gotta be like that, man. I can't handle no surprises.

Y. JACK

You played with bands?

Y. COURTENAY

Sure. Off and on...nothin' like playin' at the Casa Loma. But I've had my share of—

Y. JACK

You like to travel?

Y. COURTENAY

I'm all over the place.

Y. JACK

Nothin' to tie you down?

Y. COURTENAY

I...I go as I please, if that's what's you mean.

Y. JACK

You played with anybody you think I'd know?

Y. COURTENAY

I don't know...who do ya know?

Y. JACK

Come on—with the smart mouth...

Y. COURTENAY

I'm serious. I've played around—but I doubt you'd know who—wait: Jimmie Lunceford.

Y. JACK

You played with Jimmie Lunceford's band?

Y. COURTENAY

No—I got an uncle who played with the Delta Rhythm Boys, and he did some—

Y. JACK

From now on—you played with Jimmie Lunceford's band. For a couple of months, after the war.

Y. COURTENAY

Wait—now.

Y. JACK

Come on—Lunceford's dead. He's not talkin'. Who'll know?

Y. COURTENAY

People know. This sounds like trouble to me.

Y. JACK

Look, I'm not gettin' on my knees. I can get you in—and once you're in, I guarantee you'll travel. But we'll have to use the Lunceford thing—just to get Tiny's attention.

Y. COURTENAY

And why exactly do I want to get Mr. Stevens' attention? Come on...

Y. JACK

(Deep sigh.)
You ever had a sure thing?

Y. COURTENAY

What kinda sure thing?

Y. JACK

What I'm talkin' about here! There's nothin' like knowin' where your next pay's comin' from—and when. And there's nothin' like playin' for it. Doin' what you care about and gettin' paid for it.

Y. COURTENAY

I make my way all right.

Y. JACK
(With a bit of sarcasm.)
I'm sure you do.
(Trying to save face.)
Look, like I said I'm not gettin' down on my knees or nothin'. I just...I've never heard anybody get that kinda sound—that kinda...I mean, I've heard guys that can play a slush pump, but you...you know how to give it a voice. You deserve better than folk's pocket change.

Y. COURTENAY

So I should just pack up and follow you over to the Casa Loma, where this great big job's just sittin' there, waitin' for me...awww, man...what the hell would you do—somebody just walks up to you and...I don't even know your name.
(Y. COURTENAY and Y. JACK stare at each other for a moment, and then Y. COURTENAY kneels, scoops up the loose change, looks at it hard for a moment, grimaces, and puts it in his pocket. He then finishes putting his trombone away and closes up the case. As he rises, Y. JACK, who has been watching him, begins to speak.)

Y. JACK

I'm Jack Fornett. I'm a reed man. Clarinet. I don't know nothing about brass, except I know a good sound. And you got it...*real good.*
(Extends his hand.)

Y. COURTENAY
(After a pause, Y. COURTENAY shakes Y. JACK's hand.)
Courtenay Dees.
(Quick fade to black.)

ACT I
scene iii

(Lights up. COURTENAY's Miami Beach apartment, late 1988. A knock is heard on the door as COURTENAY plays his trombone. He goes through the melody of a Big Band tune—perhaps "Rhythm is Our Business," the theme song of Jimmie Lunceford's band. He plays low and slurs the notes together, playing only for himself...studying the song to find a line to take off from and extemporize.

There are more knocks on the door. He stops and listens, then continues playing. More aggressive knocks are heard, and then a voice.)

EUGENIA
(Offstage. Kindly, but officiously.)

Mr. Dees?

(More knocking.)

Mr. Dees—*sir.*

(More knocking. COURTENAY makes a face at the door and continues to play.)

Courtenay, you better crawl on over and answer this door. I mean it now.

(COURTENAY finishes a phrase, puts down his horn and rises to cross to the door.)

I'm gonna let myself in and you don't want that. You don't want me lettin' myself in, 'cause if I do, I'm takin' that damn noisemaker of yours, and I'm gonna place it firmly up—

(COURTENAY opens the door before she can elaborate further. EUGENIA HOLLIS is seen; a black woman in her mid-to-late fifties. She has a presence of strength about her—not necessarily because of size, but from the way she carefully carries herself. She dresses simply, in fabrics made from natural materials, in earth tones. Any jewelry she might wear would reflect an artist's handiwork. She loves to "perform," but also knows when to be genuine. As the door opens, EUGENIA briskly walks in past COURTENAY.)

Makin' me stand outside...makin' me stand in the hall like some kind of...*solicitor.*

COURTENAY
What can I do for you, Eugenia? I paid the rent on the 31st.

EUGENIA
I know you know that I knew you heard me knockin' out there. And you sit playin' that horn, just wishin' I would move on—*move on!*

COURTENAY

What can I do for you, Eugenia?

EUGENIA

Maybe I should—move on. Maybe I shouldn't do you the big favor I was doin' for you by comin' by here. And you know you paid on the 2nd, I check the box every day and nothin' came in from *you* 'til the 2nd.

COURTENAY

Maybe you didn't check that box so good.

EUGENIA

I checked that box just fine. Don't tell me about how I check boxes. I check that box *just fine.*

COURTENAY

What can I do for you, Eugenia?

EUGENIA

What can you do for me? Nothin'. Not a thing. Seems like I'm just takin' up your precious time. Excuse me for interfering with your great big excitin' life, Mr. Louis Armstrong.
          (EUGENIA makes a move to exit.)

COURTENAY

Satchmo played trumpet, Miss Hollis.

EUGENIA

Are you mocking me, Mr. Dees? I was just speaking with a metaphor.

COURTENAY

Would you like some coffee?

EUGENIA
          (Play-mocking.)
Would I like some coffee, would *I like* some coffee...

COURTENAY

Would you?

EUGENIA

Not if it's been sittin' there since Juan Valdez was born. You know I don't like that nasty dark syrupy stuff...

COURTENAY
          (In the kitchen.)
It's good coffee with chicory. You want some?

EUGENIA

That's the nasty stuff. Rates right up there with that cafe' Cubano. I like my Folger's— straight and unleaded.

COURTENAY

A real woman of the world.

EUGENIA

I could leave.

COURTENAY

You could at that.

EUGENIA

But I thought you just might like to know a little information...on the q.t., that could be helpful to you. But I'm not one to be wastin' people's time. You just keep playin' that horn of yours 'tween gulps of that nasty coffee and I'll be movin' on.

COURTENAY

Eugenia, you know I'll be glad to listen to anything you have to say.

EUGENIA
(Play-mocking.)
You'll be glad...well, I hope I'm not puttin' you out.

COURTENAY

Quit puttin' on your show and sit down. Say somethin' if you wanna say somethin'.

EUGENIA

Well, you don't have to start gettin' pushy. Lord.

COURTENAY
(Amused, shakes his head.)
You are a number you are, Miss Hollis.

EUGENIA

That I am, Mr. Dees.
(Grins. Her "performance" is obviously an encore of previous visits to his apartment.)
But now...speakin' of numbers...somebody's number's up around here. I gotta let you know— and I'm not s'posed to be openin' my mouth about this to no one, but there's gonna be some...changes...to the building. And if you think you might have trouble findin' another place to stay, I suggest you start lookin' now.

COURTENAY

What's up?

EUGENIA

We're bein' bought. Investors comin' in.

COURTENAY

Oh, Lord...Lord. I just can't rest. It's always somethin'. Always somethin'. Oh, nowwww...I guess the rent's gonna be skyrocketin'.

EUGENIA

Rent? No, this place won't be holdin' anymore tenants. There's not gonna be anybody left that stays here now...includin' me. It's set for a big change. This fine little lady comes prancing into my office today and starts explainin' how my capacity as the on-site manager will be eliminated as of the end of January. Merry Christmas and Happy New Year—this place is gonna be a flop house for the rich and famous.

COURTENAY

Another hotel.

EUGENIA

They're gonna be *preserving* the history of Miami Beach. They're comin' in here—she had *sketches*—to bring back the original *glamour* of the Art Deco District. This place is gonna be 4-star, full-service. When they finish it all up, this sad little place'll go for no less than a couple hundred a night.
(COURTENAY raises an eyebrow.)
I swear, it's true. It's gonna be restored and renewed.

COURTENAY

For who? The tourists? Not hardly anybody up and down here anymore but tourists.

EUGENIA

I'm not surprised...I knew it would be happenin'. This little place is one of the last hold-outs. In the *early* eighties, I thought—how nice, things are lookin' up around here. But I never thought that...oh, maybe I did...I knew. Oh, sure. I knew it wouldn't be long...
(Pause. She shakes her head.)

COURTENAY

So you're here till—

EUGENIA

I'm here 'till 'round the end of January. They're wantin' all of the tenants out by the *first* of January.

COURTENAY

Oh, nowwww...wait...wait, there's somethin' not quite right about that.

EUGENIA

Baby, they're the kinda folks that can do what it is they want to do...they talk the talk.

(Rubs her fingers together indicating money.)

COURTENAY

So you're saying I got about three weeks here? That everybody here's got less than a month to--

EUGENIA

That's what I'm sayin'.

COURTENAY

No...no, this isn't right. Noooo...and not givin' us notice...what is all this?

EUGENIA

At the end of this week, everybody's gonna get *these* little notices.
                    (Takes a notice out of her pocket.)
See here.
                    (Pointing out print on the notice.)
Your rent's all set to triple if ya stay. And some of the larger units—quadruple. That's how they're gonna have this place cleared out. They *know* nobody here can pay that no how.

COURTENAY

I tell ya, this isn't right.

EUGENIA

When has anything ever been right?

COURTENAY

No, I mean this is illegal not kinda right.

EUGENIA

Legal, illegal, they'll do what they please. Don't they always? 'Fore next year is out, this little place'll be 4 star, full-service.

COURTENAY
                    (COURTENAY thinks hard for a moment.)
Mmhh. Well...
                    (He sighs and shakes his head in frustration.)

EUGENIA

I'm supposed to be real sly about all of this...the little lady says I'll get a nice severance package from the property company if I just keep doin' what I'm doin' and take an order when they wanna hand it down. Help them make the—
                    (The little lady's words.)
"...transition a smooth process for everyone." Transition. *Eviction.*

COURTENAY

You gonna let anybody else know about all this?

EUGENIA
(Serious, perplexed. A little at sea.)
I don't...I don't quite really know *what* to do, Court.

COURTENAY
You told *me*.

EUGENIA
Uhm. Yeah.

COURTENAY
(Also somewhat at sea.)
I appreciate the information.

EUGENIA
I'm sure you do. But, you know, lookin' around here, a person woulda thought you seen it comin'. Eight months and it hardly looks like you've ever got real ambitious about unpackin'.
(EUGENIA points to the trunk and all the items sprawled atop it.)
You got yourself a skeleton in that trunk, Mr. Dees? What're you hidin' in there?

COURTENAY
My stuff. Everybody's got stuff. No sense in draggin' it out all over the place.
(There is a long pause. COURTENAY hangs his head in the quiet.)

EUGENIA
Well...I guess you won't be havin' to listen to me beat your door down at the top of the month anymore—shakin' you down...
(The quiet resumes; conversation has come to an end. Begins to exit.)
I guess we both got our thinkin' to do.

COURTENAY
I guess so.

EUGENIA
Well...if you have any real fine ideas about anything, you know where I am.

COURTENAY
Uhm-hmm.
(Sits still, thinking.)

EUGENIA
(Facetiously, as she goes to the door to let herself out.)
No, now don't bother bein' half-human and showing me to the door, I know the way. I don't need any special treatment. Don't strain yourself, man.
(He rises to go to the door, but EUGENIA exits before he can show her out. He watches her go. After a moment, he goes to his trombone.

He starts to bring it to his lips and then stops. He looks hard at the horn, and then looks out—and up.)

COURTENAY

You always said I couldn't sit still even if I wanted to...and now when I want to, and need to, you're right...even now I can't, Jewel...can't sit still even when I want to...*can't—just—sit—still...*

(Lights slowly fade to black.)

ACT I
scene iv

(Lights up. 1948. A slide projection reflects St. Louis' Casa Loma Ballroom; empty. Little, if any, set dressing complements this black and white image. YOUNG JACK speaks, impassioned, to someone very real—but unseen by the audience.)

Y. JACK

Lunceford...yeah—talk to him about it. Or better yet, Tiny, just listen to him play. He's got it. I mean—the boy doesn't just know his horn, it's like a part of him. I was over to Union Station a couple of days ago, and I heard—now look—I'm not going goofy on ya here. All I can say is, you gotta hear him. I don't gotta sell him to you—'cause, you know—Tiny, when Fred's gone, he's gone—we gotta do *somethin'* before we leave for Hot Springs. No, I'm not tellin' anybody their business, it's just that...look: when we play The Arlington, we gotta have *somebody*, we gotta shine when we got a gig like that on our hands. Yeah, I know you know how to run the— I'm well aware. Yeah, I've thought about that, but, Tine—if it's just a question of that—is it just a question of *that?* The other guys'll be fine about it. I just know. 'Cause I just know. Okay—I took a little poll about it—yeah, I talked to the other guys—so shoot me—I took a sampling— and nobody cares. Nobody thinks about it—it's the *sound* that matters and Tine, I mean, listen: let's get practical here...you say it all the time—you're a businessman, this is a business. Think of this: you won't have to fork over Fred's salary...*half* of it—I'm sure, Tine—*half*—it's probably more than the guy's ever seen at once...um-hmmmm...*no*, he won't know. No—no way would I discuss money with him, Tine—that's your angle, that's all yours, I respect that. Trouble? You just gotta trust me on this one—he won't cause any trouble, all he wants to do is play. Just...just you listen to him, Tiny, just listen. Let me tell him you'll give him five minutes and then I'll shut up, it'll all be up to you, I won't say another word on it, the horn can do all the talking. Five minutes... whaddaya say?

(Lights fade quickly to black.)

ACT I
scene v

(Lights up. COURTENAY's Miami Beach apartment, late 1988. COURTENAY is seen struggling to write a letter. He tries sitting or standing in different areas of the small apartment to find some level of comfort in order to allow his thoughts to flow. He finally sits at the eating area and reviews a completed draft of the letter with which he has been struggling.)

COURTENAY
(Reading from the paper, making changes as he goes along.)

*Dear Mr. Davies...*Mr. Davies, no...*Dear William. Your call was not unwelcome. If I seemed...*no, just...*I hope you have some good fortune finding the whereabouts of your father.* Yeah. *As I told you, it has been many years since your father and I worked together.* Let's see now...

(COURTENAY sighs, trying to recall.)

After giving it some thought, I believe the last I heard of Jack...was in the early fifties...something about a gig in New Rochelle. I'm sure by then his big dream was spent and gone.

(COURTENAY's eyes grow big.)

Oh God, no. The kid'll pull a Hemingway if he reads that. Just...*Last I heard he* was *playing in New Rochelle. But I'm sure someone pointed the way outta there for him by now. I'd be glad to talk to you more, but there's really not much more to say. I have to say I'm puzzled...*no. Impressed? *I'm surprised by your knowledge of me. I knew little of your mother.* No. *Your mother was a fine woman, and I'm flattered she spoke of me. My condolences on her—*no, no talkin' about death. *I wish I could be more help to you, but my memories of Jack and your mother are...*no. God, I can't even remember that woman's name. Lou? Lou Ellen? Aw, skip it...just skip it...

(COURTENAY stops, and is lost in thought for a moment. He puts down the paper and stands. He is troubled. He goes to the open window in the kitchen and stares out, listening to the street sounds of Miami Beach. He re-enters the living area and turns his radio on at a low volume; a slow jazz instrumental of a Christmas tune plays. He then returns to write a final draft of the letter; he writes, then reads it aloud.)

Dear William. I hope you have good fortune finding your father. Truly, Courtenay Dees.

(COURTENAY looks at the brief note for a moment, and appears satisfied with its content. Lights fade to black.)

(Lights up. 1948. A slide projection reflects the main entrance/veranda of The Arlington in Hot Springs, Arkansas. Little, if any, set dressing complements this black and white image— perhaps only some outdoor furniture. YOUNG JACK, with his clarinet case nearby, speaks with LOLA RAE ALLEN, a lovely young girl of 20—though looking somewhat younger than her actual age. She has only a trace of a Southern dialect. They are in the middle of conversation.)

Y. JACK

Oh...I didn't serve in the war in the—I guess what you'd say—the usual sense. Ever heard of noncombat war service?

LOLA RAE

War service...what's that?

Y. JACK

Didn't you have any friends or—you had to've had friends or family in the war.

LOLA RAE

My stepbrother fought in the war, and cousins.

Y. JACK

You never heard of—

LOLA RAE

I've never had a lot of patience for talking about the war. I guess that's real bad of me, huh? But I'm not like a Communist or anything.

Y. JACK

Wouldn't have pegged you as one in a million years.

LOLA RAE
(Worried that she has appeared callous.)
I like being American. A lot.

Y. JACK

And so do I—so do I. That's why, baby doll, I did my good turn for Uncle Sam, right here, during the war. Because I'm proud to call myself an—oh—but now keep in mind, this is highly classified. I really can't go into a lotta detail.

LOLA RAE

Oh. I wouldn't ask you—

Y. JACK

Won't even be able to share the stories with my grandkids someday. I don't want to say I was workin' top secret—but, you know—highly classified stuff. Can't exactly go talking about it with anyone.

LOLA RAE

Of course.

Y. JACK
(Smiles, amused with himself.)
Sooo, uh—you wanna come up to my room tonight after the show?

LOLA RAE

Jack!

Y. JACK

Just to kick back.

LOLA RAE
(Grinning, but uncomfortable.)
Jack, I don't think so.

Y. JACK

Hey, I'm just kiddin' around with you. Musicians kid around—can't take anything we say too seriously.

LOLA RAE

Well, you're the first musician I've ever really known. I'll have to try to keep that in mind.

Y. JACK

If you know what's healthy for you. Heyyyy, wait a minute. You got musicians comin' and goin' outta here all the time. You tellin' me here you've never gotten too friendly with one of the guys before?

LOLA RAE

I've never really...you see, like you said about not taking things too seriously...that's probably real good, 'cause I'm—well, I'm kind of engaged.

Y. JACK

What do you mean—kind of engaged?

LOLA RAE

I have a fiance'.

                            Y. JACK
In a fifty mile radius of here?

                            LOLA RAE
Just down the street—at The Majestic. He works front desk.

                            Y. JACK
Ooooh. Well, Lola Rae Allen—good to meet ya, but I'm not what you'd call a competitive guy.

                            LOLA RAE
No, now, don't start actin' nervous. He's just this sweet, hard working guy—from Texas. Billy Odell Davies.

                            Y. JACK
                    (Struck by the odd name.)
Billy Odell?

                            LOLA RAE
I think it's a Texas thing. Anyway, all the girls around here have some kind of steady guy...and a girlfriend of mine introduced me to him. He kept hanging around, hanging around the barber shop, gettin' manicures with me all the time. I finally told him that I'm sure the shop needed the business, but it was gettin' embarrassin' doin' his nails *everyday*, sometimes twice.

                            Y. JACK
He *must* be nuts about you. Or just nuts.

                            LOLA RAE
So he stopped gettin' his nails done and started askin' me out, and earlier this year he asked me to marry him. See?
                    (Shows off a small diamond ring.)

                            Y. JACK
So what're you doin' have drinks with me after the show, showin' me around, and makin' so nice?

                            LOLA RAE
Maybe you're about the most interesting guy I've ever met—who's showed a little interest in me.

                            Y. JACK
Well, I am an interestin' guy, but baby doll, if you got a fiance'—

                            LOLA RAE
Jack...Jack, you're a real good time. And I *know* you'll only be here a coupla weeks more. I can keep things quiet. Let's just...if you wanna keep seein' me, it'd mean a lot to me. Like you said—about not takin' things too seriously, I promise I can do that.

Y. JACK

Oh, nowwww...you're just a kid, you don't need to be—

LOLA RAE

A kid? I'm twenty.

Y. JACK

You're just a kid.

LOLA RAE

And what are you—a hundred?

Y. JACK

I'm twenty-five, and I've been around a little more than you, cherub. I've seen a little more life—and I know...

LOLA RAE

What do you know?

Y. JACK

I know somethin' like this could mess up things for you here. *You know*—two weeks and I'm gone. What if Billy Bob finds out about us? Your bright little future would be—

LOLA RAE

I wish I would've never said anything about him. Can't we forget that I ever said anything— Jack? Maybe you and I—we could just be good friends—just pal around while you're here. I like you—I like your smile, and your stories. I like to hear about...

Y. JACK

Oh, don't start whinin'. And lookin' sad. Don't start that. I'll do anything if you don't start that.

LOLA RAE

Then tell me again about the band you're startin'—and the places you're gonna go to and play and—and about the celebrity people you know, and—

Y. JACK

(He reaches out with his index finger and places it across her lips to gently hush her.)
Shhhh...you want to hear my stories. I'll tell them to you. I'll sit here and look in those wonderful sweet eyes of yours and tell them all to you. But this Bubba of yours, you gotta—

LOLA RAE

Billy Odell. And for the next two weeks, he just doesn't exist. Don't worry. I can handle it.

Y. JACK

Little Miss Arkansas can handle it. Just what else can you handle, Lola Rae?

LOLA RAE

Whatever I have a mind to.

Y. JACK

I think I like the sound of that.

LOLA RAE

Yeah, I bet you do. Just don't go expectin' too much.

Y. JACK

Too much is barely enough.
                    (He leans in and kisses her.)

LOLA RAE
                    (After the kiss.)
Hey...hey, you think maybe we can do a double date some night with you and your friend—ohh,
what's his name? In the band.

Y. JACK

There's a lotta guys in the band.

LOLA RAE

Plays the trombone, you said you wanted to start your own band with him.

Y. JACK

Courtenay. Well, we got a nice workin' relationship...we're even working on our own song. But
outside of the music, we pretty much keep to ourselves. He's colored.

LOLA RAE
                    (Struck by Y. JACK's comment/tone.)
Welllll, Jack—

Y. JACK

Well, Jack what—?

LOLA RAE

I gotta—one of my girlfriends...she's colored. We get along fine. She works here in the hotel.

Y. JACK

Well...maybe things are different around here, but where I come from...

LOLA RAE

Oh, Jack.

Y. JACK

I was born in Kansas, and all I can say is...people there—

LOLA RAE

Oh, now, don't go draggin' the whole state of Kansas into—

Y. JACK

Hey—hey, there...things are nice. Let's just—let's keep 'em that way, huh?
(Looking into her eyes, romancing her.)
We got two weeks, they could be great. Let's not—ya know what I mean…let's keep things simple.
(LOLA RAE looks away, somewhat shyly, somewhat unsure. He gently
turns her face to back to him.)
Hey...you know, you've got the greatest eyes. Beautiful sparkles. Yeah. A guy could write a
song. Sure...about Little Miss Arkansas. You think you'd like your own hit song?

LOLA RAE

(Softly.)
I think I would, Jack. I think I really would.
(He kisses her deeply as the lights fade to black.)

ACT I
scene vii

(Lights up. COURTENAY's Miami Beach apartment, late 1988. A large cardboard box is placed in a central location in the apartment; it is obvious that COURTENAY has started to pack things away for the move. The trunk has been mostly uncovered—and is now more visible. COURTENAY is seen on his back asleep on the sofa; he appears unkempt. The radio plays at a low volume.)

RADIO BROADCASTER 2
(A female voice with Mid-American dialect.)
And retailers are hopeful that the holiday season will see increased spending among consumers. In international news, Benazir Bhutto—
(There is a knock on the door; COURTENAY begins to stir.)

EUGENIA
(Offstage.)
Court, you gotta come outta there sometime. Haven't heard nothin' of you in almost—is that the radio?
(More knocks. COURTENAY begins to reluctantly rise.)
Mr. Dees, if you don't answer your door, I'm gonna have to let myself in with the pass key. I am legally entitled to make sure the tenants are up and breathin'. You hear me, man? Are you breathin'?

RADIO BROADCASTER 2
—daughter of former prime minister Zulfikar Ali Bhutto, has been elected prime minister of Pakistan. Bhutto is the first woman to head a modern Islamic state, and her election brings eleven years of military rule to an end. In South Africa, Charles Bester, an eighteen- year-old white South African has been sentenced to six years in prison for refusing conscription into the South African Defense force. A committed pacifist, Bester stated--

(COURTENAY turns off the radio and goes to the door.)

EUGENIA
I'm countin' to ten, man, and then I'm in there. Hear? One—
(COURTENAY opens the door.)

COURTENAY
Why can't you just let a person be?

EUGENIA
Why can't you just answer the door like some normal person?

COURTENAY

I'm resting, Eugenia.

EUGENIA

I was, honest to God, more than half expectin' to come in here and find you stone cold. Nobody's seen you come in or out in three days. How're you gonna get by without...*restin's* not gonna bring in any grocery money.

COURTENAY

What do you care about my grocery money? I'm not any of your business.

EUGENIA

Oh, nowww. Don't go talking so hateful. You know I care if my tenants eat. And I know if you're not outta here every evenin' by six or seven, that you're gonna be down to makin' hard choices about eatin'. You've been holed up in here since I talked to ya last.

COURTENAY

I've decided I'm retirin'. I'm in retirement.

EUGENIA

What the hell is retirement? What's wrong with you?

COURTENAY

I just need some time to myself.

EUGENIA

(Surveys his attempts at packing. Begins to understand.)

Time to get sick and depressed. That's all time to yourself is good for.

COURTENAY

You think so?

EUGENIA

Well, look at you. No, don't look at you—you might get a shock. Is it the shower you've retired from? What's wrong with you, man?

COURTENAY

I'm fine, I'm fine—it's just people messin' with me.

EUGENIA

Well...God forbid that I—*pardon me*—

(She makes a move to exit.)

COURTENAY

(Stopping her.)

No—nowwww. Don't. 'Gen—just...don't.

EUGENIA
(She looks hard at him.)
Court...I know this movin' thing...it's got me down, too. And I'm torn up by it. I feel like like...I feel like I'm turnin' my back on all the tenants, but what is it that I can do to change anything? I got a lot on my mind here, too--but I'm still bathin'.

COURTENAY
No, it's not just the move that's got me—it's not *just* that...it's a whole lotta...
(Shakes his head. A pause.)

EUGENIA
Listen: I'll sit here, I'll drink some of that mud in a cup a'yours—just to be sociable—and I'll be the finest listener, if you can come out of retirement long enough to tell me what's bitin' you in the head.

COURTENAY
(Going to the kitchen to make his coffee with chicory.)
I just...I've been thinkin' over a lotta things the past coupla days. Things that I thought were ancient history. Things I thought were long over and done. All done. Things I thought were *so* over and done with that...

EUGENIA
You're talkin' in circles, man.

COURTENAY
And thinkin' in circles...and feelin'...havin' feelin's I could just as well do without. Just a whole lotta hurtfulness.

EUGENIA
(Straightforward.)
What's wrong with you, Courtenay?

COURTENAY
(After a beat.)
I got a call. From a boy looking for his father.

EUGENIA
You got children out there somewhere?

COURTENAY
Oh God, no. Well, not that I know anything about. His father was a man I...I knew his father back in '48, for just a short time. And his mother—I knew the boy's mother...barely.
(Shakes his head, somewhat lost, torn by the memories.)
But it's been forty years. And...he wanted to know anything, *anything* I could pass on that'd help him find his father.
(A small laugh at himself.)

COURTENAY cont'd

I call him a boy—he must be...
(It occurs to him.)
thirty-nine years old.

EUGENIA

So his mother's no help in findin' his father?

COURTENAY

It didn't work out with the father. And now his mother's passed on.

EUGENIA

Well, did you straight out tell him you couldn't help him?

COURTENAY

Yeah, I told him, but even so he kept me on the phone for more than half an hour. He was just so excited to have found some kind of—contact. He was so sure there had to be something I knew that would...said he'd be checkin' back with me to see if I remembered anything. He gave me his address and fax and home phone, work phone, car phone, sayin' *just in case*, but there's nothing. I don't have nothin' for him.

EUGENIA

So why's somebody else's son got you down?

COURTENAY

There's a whole lot tied into him that...there's a whole lotta things there I thought I'd never have to have any kinda thoughts or feelin's about ever again. And that's the way that I wanted it. That was fine by me.

EUGENIA

But now you're stuck with somethin'.

COURTENAY

(As the coffee brews, he enters the living area.)
Stuck with a whole lotta uselessness—things I can't do anything with or about. And now I'm packin' to go to nowhere. I imagine this is gonna be the wickedest Christmas I've ever seen.

EUGENIA

Don't sacrilege.

COURTENAY

I got somethin'...all 'round me now...somethin' that's so...stiflin'. It like it's...eatin' into all my thoughts and takin' the air that I wanna breathe.

EUGENIA

You got some unfinished business?

COURTENAY
(Kneels before the trunk looking at the stickers identifying past travels,
And running his fingers over the découpage.)
It's not my business. It's just history.

EUGENIA
Sounds like whether you think so or not, it's your business.

COURTENAY
I'm not claimin' it as my business.

EUGENIA
You don't have to, man. It's claimed *you.* It's claimed you good.

COURTENAY
(Staring at the trunk. There is a pause. He quotes poetry, *slowly*, in a low
voice, almost a mumble:)
"I would liken you
To a night without stars
Were it not for your eyes.
I would liken you
To a sleep without dreams..."
(He stops, lost in a memory.)

EUGENIA
(After an uncomfortable pause.)
Now...forgive me for not appearing grateful—but are you askin' me to stay for more than coffee?

COURTENAY
(Abruptly rises from the trunk.)
That's Langston Hughes, Miss Hollis. You should know Langston Hughes. I had somebody once
who had a head full of his words—and now, when it doesn't do me much good at all, I
remember.
(Crosses to the kitchen for coffee as EUGENIA stares at the trunk.)
You're gonna have a cup of my coffee?
(He begins to pour coffee. She rises and slowly goes to get a better look
at the trunk.)

EUGENIA
You been to all these places—these places on this trunk?

COURTENAY
(Affirmatively.)
Uhm-hmmm.

EUGENIA

Looks like a relic. You drag it with you everywhere you stay?

(Looks at the rusted lock fastening the trunk shut; shakes it.)

When were you in it last?

(COURTENAY doesn't respond.)

You know, you should go through it. Make sure, you know, anything precious is still—

COURTENAY

The key's gone—been gone, for I don't know how long.

EUGENIA

You could open it if you wanted to.

COURTENAY

Trunk doesn't need to be opened.

EUGENIA

I'm just sayin'—even with the key bein' gone, you could still—you could get yourself some kinda tool and open it.

COURTENAY

Trunk's fine the way it is, Gen. Get on away from the trunk, now.

EUGENIA

I'm just saying—some kinda *tool*—

COURTENAY

(Deliberately changing the subject.)

I forget—you take sugar? Some milk?

EUGENIA

(Understanding. After a beat:)

Anything to calm it down.

COURTENAY

(Prepares her coffee.)

I'm sorry for gettin' you all concerned about me, Eugenia. I just gotta...gotta get my head straight. Got some things that I...

EUGENIA

I know. We all got some things.

(COURTENAY gives her the coffee.)

You know, I don't *mean* to be in your business. Wouldn't have made any kinda fuss, but this morning I realized I hadn't heard that noisemaker of yours in seventy-two hours. That's what got me. It just seemed...not right. *Not right* around here without that sound of yours.

COURTENAY

That sound of mine.

EUGENIA

Gives the building some personality, gives it spirit. Lets folks know that people *live* here.
>   (They connect, and COURTENAY smiles. She then reaches for the coffee
>   and begins to sip. Immediately, she curls her lips at the taste. As typical,
>   her response is theatrical.)

Ohhh...I am *so* sorry. *Oh.* I thought I might could stand it, but...ooooh.

COURTENAY

>   (Incredulous.)

Now *how* can you—that's good coffee--how can you not like that?

EUGENIA

>   (She smacks her mouth, trying to rid it of the rich but bitter taste. She
>   makes an awful face.)

I don't know...but I *do not* like that. *Oh!*
>   (He laughs at her theatrics as the lights fade to black.)

ACT I
scene viii

(Lights up. 1948. A slide projection reflects an image of the grand, but empty, Crystal Ballroom in The Arlington. Little, if any, set dressing complements this black and white image. YOUNG JACK and YOUNG COURTENAY are developing/rehearsing their song.)

Y. COURTENAY
(After playing a stretch for Y. JACK to consider.)
I think it'd be closer to...I think it needs *your* sound, Jack.

Y. JACK
No, I told ya, I like what you're doin'...I'll follow along. Go on—start in again...

Y. COURTENAY
I'm tellin' ya—give it a shot.

Y. JACK
Just play as written, Court.
(Y. COURTENAY, uneasily, begins again. Y. JACK speaks as Y. COURTENAY plays.)

Y. JACK
That's it...that's it...now I can come in with some...
(Y. JACK plays, complementing Y. COURTENAY on the melody line. Y. COURTENAY's melody begins to become looser, freer—more like jazz than a big band melody line. Y. JACK stops.)
Aww, come on...

Y. COURTENAY
What? We were doin' fine...

Y. JACK
That's great, but it's not what were workin' on here. Like I told you in St. Louis, I'm looking for something with that kinda feel, but people gotta feel like they can dance to it, Court. What the hell are ya doin' here?

Y. COURTENAY
Listen...let *me* follow *you*. I know what you're lookin' for, and—

Y. JACK
This song's gonna feature *you*, it's gonna show off that sound of yours.

                    Y. COURTENAY
Just once, for kicks—

                    Y. JACK
Come on, we don't have much time. They're gonna be settin' up for some shindig in here. Play.

                    Y. COURTENAY
Just hear me out.

                    Y. JACK
Wastin' time...

                    Y. COURTENAY
Take the melody line and let *me* follow.

                    Y. JACK
What are you talking about? We almost got somethin' here.

                    Y. COURTENAY
I know what we got, but I think we could have somethin' better.

                    Y. JACK
Court. Listen. Just shut up and play. We're never gonna get anywhere with you mouthin' off.

                    Y. COURTENAY
            (After a beat.)
What's got into you, man?

                    Y. JACK
What's got into me? We almost got somethin' here and—look—you said—you said you were interested in doin' somethin'. And you know, I'm out to make things happen. If you wanna be a part of 'em, ya gotta go with me. Compromise is for the birds. No compromises. And no smart mouth. I call the shots here. Now play. As written.
            (Y. COURTENAY *slowly* puts down his horn; anger and frustration well up inside of him.)
Is there somethin' you need to say to me? 'Cause if there is, you do it now. Don't go stringin' along—say it now. I don't wanna lotta trouble, I just want to work. I wanna make somethin'. I thought you wanted somethin' like that, too.

                    Y. COURTENAY
            (He breathes deeply, and then puts on a pleasant persona.)
I'm—uh...I guess—it's just the heat, man. I can't think. The heat must be gettin' to me.

                    Y. JACK
The heat...July in lovely Hot Springs, Arkansas. You'll be fine, just take a breather.

Y. COURTENAY

Maybe we oughta go take a breather outside...its stiflin' in here.

Y. JACK

Just relax for a minute—we're so close—let's stick it out till we got something *real* finished.

Y. COURTENAY

I *am* real finished. Look, we been goin' at it for near to four hours today. We're not gonna have any chops left for tonight. I'm not tellin' you your business, I'm just sayin'—gotta take things a step at a time. We gotta gig tonight, somethin' to be thankful for, and we gotta meet that.

Y. JACK

Hey...look...ya know...I'm not really interested in whether I got somethin' for Tiny Stevens tonight or not. I mean, don't misunderstand—I gotta certain amount of loyalty to the guy, and to the band, but I gotta get real serious with ya here: I got to go after somethin' myself. And I see you bein' a part of it. The first time I heard you play, you just messin' around on the street, I thought, when I build my own combo that's the kinda sound I want. Ya gotta...I want you to understand now...it's...when I hear the names—when I hear somebody say Isham Jones or Harry James, Artie Shaw...Gene Krupa...I think to myself, hell—if those clowns can call their own shots, then why not me, huh?
(In his head, dream-like.)
Sure. That's what it's all about. Callin' the shots. Being a big cat and havin' a name. Household name...
(Directly to Y. COURTENAY.)
Do ya see? Ya see what I'm sayin', Court?

Y. COURTENAY
(Trying to diffuse the tension.)

Yeah.

Y. JACK

Yeah...
(As if he is about to speak further—but lets the idea go.)

Y. COURTENAY
(After a pause.)

So I..guess I gotta keep remindin' myself, I'm workin' under General Patton here. Gotta get the job done, no bellyachin'.

Y. JACK

No, I'm not draggin' anybody into combat here...you're only with me if you wanna be.

Y. COURTENAY

I'm not ever anywhere I don't wanna be.

Y. JACK

Okay. Okay...so we got it all straight.

Y. COURTENAY

For now.

Y, JACK

(LOLA RAE enters the ballroom.)

For now...that's the problem here.

(Y. JACK spies LOLA RAE, then finishes his thought.)

I've been talking about somethin' a lot bigger than *just now*.

LOLA RAE

Hey there. Is this a good time?

Y. JACK

So you following me around like a puppy dog now?

LOLA RAE

No. I just—when I was on my break earlier today I could hear this playin', music driftin' all the way down to the shopping arcade. I was thinking it was you and—

Y. JACK

And here we are.

(LOLA RAE makes a gesture that she would like to be introduced to Y. COURTENAY.)

Oh. Courtenay Dees, Lola Rae Allen. Lola Rae Allen...

Y. COURTENAY

Pleased to meet you, Miss Allen.

LOLA RAE

If you call me Miss Allen, I'll have to call you Mr. Dees—and I really think that's much too formal.

Y. COURTENAY

Good to meet you, Lola Rae.

LOLA RAE

Good to meet you, Courtenay. Jack's spoken of you.

Y. JACK

Lola Rae—we're kinda on the clock here.

LOLA RAE

Oh—yeah—okay. I just...you know, Courtenay—I was just tellin' Jack that, well—it might be

LOLA RAE cont'd

fun to have a couple of laughs before you guys leave town. There's a girl I know here at the hotel, and there's this club where—

Y. COURTENAY

I have to say I'm already spoken for, Miss—Lola Rae.

Y. JACK

Courtenay's not interested in socializing, Lola Rae. Look, why don't you and I—why don't we have a little dinner together before the show.

LOLA RAE

I'm sorry. I interrupted your work. I really didn't mean—

Y. JACK
(Trying to show her out.)
No, now—don't go bein' sorry—just meet me round 5:30—

LOLA RAE

There's a place down past the bathhouses. You can get catfish dinners for seventy-five cents.

Y. JACK

That's fine. That's just fine.

LOLA RAE

Courtenay, would you like us to bring you back something?

Y. COURTENAY

Thank you, but I'm headin' back up the road to where I'm stayin'—catch a little rest. I'll get supper there.

LOLA RAE
(To Y. COURTENAY.)
Are you comfortable where you are? 'Cause at my house, we got an extra room, it's all made up—and—

Y. JACK

Lola—*please.* My God.

Y. COURTENAY

Mr. Stevens got me set up at the National, Lola Rae. I'm fine.

Y. JACK

You know, Lola—you and I, we had this talk—remember? Simple?

LOLA RAE

I know, Jack.

Y. JACK

So what are you doin' here? Are we plannin' ourselves a dinner for tonight, or are you in the mood to cause big trouble for Courtenay?

LOLA RAE
(After a beat.)
Oh. I didn't—I don't mean to—

Y. COURTENAY

You have your catfish dinner with Jack, Lola Rae.

Y. JACK

I'll meet you in the lobby at 5:30. We'll go to this place of yours.

LOLA RAE

Yeah...

Y. JACK

Have a catfish. It'll be great.

LOLA RAE

Yeah. It'll be all right.

Y. JACK

5:30.
(She turns to go.)
Hey—hey there—slow down.
(He grabs her, turning her to him.)
Let me see those big brown eyes.
(He gives her a quick peck on the cheek. She smiles—but with an uncertainty. She begins to exit.)

LOLA RAE
(Turning to Y. COURTENAY.)
I'm glad to've gotten to meet you, Courtenay. I'm sorry for...

Y. COURTENAY
(Trying to put her at ease. Gracefully.)
I'll see you around, Lola Rae.

LOLA RAE

Yeah. Thanks.
(LOLA RAE exits the ballroom.)

Y. JACK
(An afterthought, to LOLA RAE.)
Hey—and maybe after the show—Lola...maybe after—
(But she is gone. He gives a deep, tired sigh as he turns to face
Y. COURTENAY.)
I tell ya...she's a cute little thing, but...

Y. COURTENAY
She didn't mean anything.

Y. JACK
She's gotta know her place. We had this talk a couple of days ago—I thought she understood
how things had to be if she wanted to—
(Y. JACK pauses, lost in thought.)

Y. COURTENAY
You wanna finish up here?

Y. JACK
You ever had to...you ever had trouble with a girl? On the road. I mean, lettin' her know how
things stand?

Y. COURTENAY
I-uhh...I've had my share of headaches. Who hasn't?

Y. JACK
Yeah...who hasn't? So...uh—yeah—let's finish up. Let's uh...

Y. COURTENAY
I'll start out at the top?

Y. JACK
Sure. Just—uh...
(JACK pauses.)

Y. COURTENAY
Just—uh, *what?*

Y. JACK
Why don't...why don't you show me what you have in mind.

Y. COURTENAY
About you on the—

Y. JACK
Yeah, yeah—I'll take the melody—what the hell—to see what it sounds like.

Y. COURTENAY

Wait, now. You *wanna* take the melody line?

Y. JACK

I just want...for it sell. That's all. I just...let's just let the music do the talkin'. If it's got the right sound, then there won't be any arguing with it.

Y. COURTENAY

So you *want* to take the melody line. You are somethin' to figure out, Jack Fornett.

Y. JACK

Come on...

Y. COURTENAY

You think you got it?

Y. JACK

Sure, in my sleep. Just—uh...I'll start. You do whatever it is that—

Y. COURTENAY

I'll take it—but ya gotta let it ride. No corn. Just kick it out.

Y. JACK

(The young men get set to record again, with Y. JACK waving to the booth to get a go ahead.)

I got it, I got it. You just hang onto your horn.

(Fade to black.)

ACT I
scene ix

(Lights up. COURTENAY's Miami Beach apartment, late 1988. COURTENAY's packing has not progressed much from the last scene. He enters from the "bathroom" area, having just taken a shower. He wears pants and socks, and is putting on a handsome shirt in a bold color. He is quoting lyrics, roughly and slowly, from an old Cab Calloway tune, *Some of These Days*; he half sings, half speaks. He moves through the apartment to find his shoes and a belt. Whenever he passes the trunk, he considers it—perhaps with a glance, perhaps with a stare, perhaps by raising an eyebrow—or a combination of these.)

COURTENAY

"Some of these days
You're gonna be so lonely
Some of these days
You're gonna want me only
Yoooou will miss my lovin'
Miss my kisses
You're gonna miss your little Daddy
When he goes away..."

(COURTENAY he stops abruptly in front of the trunk, and stares at it hard. As he stares, JEWEL enters, a young black woman in her mid-twenties. She is pure energy and memory—not a "ghost." She is youth and joy. Her costume reflects the dress of a schoolteacher, living modestly in the late '40s. Her hair is straightened and pulled back into a bun at the nape of her neck. She wears make-up, applied by a young woman wanting to appear "worldly" for a special occasion; it does not, however, detract from her gentle charm. She enters from a place not within COURTENAY's apartment proper, but from somewhere on the fringes of the set. She works her way—is drawn—to COURTENAY. <u>She is **never** perceived by him</u>; he begins to speak—full attention on the trunk.)

A man with two loves who never considered himself to be unfaithful. A man who can bury the best woman who ever lived, who ever loved him, and not shed a tear for her—even though he's torn up in pieces inside...'cause he knows...a little bit of her died so long ago, so long before she ever got sick, 'cause he couldn't do right by her.

(Sits on the trunk; his focus changes to up and out.)

You tried telling me...you didn't need the money. Every month when I'd send you money, you knew I was really trying to send away the guilt, huh? What else did you know? You knew I had the wanderlust...no, more than that...not a lust, a real love...love that was as strong...as strong as my love for you.

COURTENAY cont'd
(Buries his head in his hands for a moment. When looks up, JEWEL is
very near him.)

I did you love you, Jewel. With your head all full of wise things and poetry. I do still love
you...even now, when it does the both of us no good. It does me no good, just like keepin' up
with this trunk. No good. You were my schoolteacher, always teachin'. What was it that I needed
to learn? What was it that I never learned, 'cause it's something, baby. It's something so big,
something that could keep me and haunt me for all these years after you've gone. Carry you
around in my head, but never be able to shed a real tear and let ya go. My schoolteacher...hat was
it you wanted me to learn?

(He puts on his shoes in the quiet, and then looks at his reflection in a
small mirror hanging on the wall. He smiles—remembering an afternoon
long ago with JEWEL; it inspires another Cab Calloway tribute.)

"...when you walk down the avenue
All the folks just can't believe it's you..."

(COURTENAY passes within inches of JEWEL as he continues getting
ready. She begins to exit out of his apartment proper, disappearing past the
fringes of the set and sightlines.)

"With all those painted lips, and painted eyes...
Wearing a bird of paradise..."

(He stops, in mid-lyric/mid-thought, and then goes to the door. He leans
his head back, inhales deeply, and sighs. He goes out, fairly slamming the
door behind him. After a brief moment, the phone begins to ring again.
Fade to black.)

ACT I
scene x

(Lights up. 1948. A slide projection reflects bathhouse row in Hot Springs, Arkansas. A wrought iron bench and little more, if any, set dressing complements this black and white image. YOUNG COURTENAY is seen eating the last of an ice cream cone, leaning over the bench. JEWEL finishes a cone as well; she wears the same costume seen in the previous scene, plus a pocketbook and a prim hat—with a bird of paradise.)

Y. COURTENAY

So, you think you'll have some good kids when it starts up again?

JEWEL

Oh, every year, they're always precious. I'm gonna have Leona Redding's twin boys this time around.

Y. COURTENAY

They're goin' into second grade already? Nooo...

JEWEL

Yes.

Y. COURTENAY

Those two little—

JEWEL

Little? They're already chest high to Leona—which I guess isn't saying much, but they're gonna be tall boys. They look so much like Joseph—gonna be big, tall and handsome, just like him.

Y. COURTENAY

She doin' okay?

JEWEL

Oh. I don't think she'll ever be *okay*, but she gets by. You know, when I get to mopin' about you bein' gone all the time she says to me—not cryin', just real strong—she says—*at least he's under the same moon and stars that you are*...and that I should count my blessings, everyday, that you came back to me from the war. And I do.

Y. COURTENAY

And you gotta believe I do, too.

JEWEL

Yes...thank God you came back from the 93rd Infantry—so that I can follow you all over the United States in a Greyhound bus.

Y. COURTENAY

Oh..nooowww. Let's not start...
(She raises an eyebrow at him.)
Why don't we talk about your—uh...

JEWEL
(Putting him on the spot for changing the subject.)

Umm-hmmm?

Y. COURTENAY
(Pleased he has thought of a new subject.)
Your Sunday School class. You still got your Sunday School kids?

JEWEL
(Going along.)
I do. Got a new group beginning of summer.

Y. COURTENAY

Got all angels?

JEWEL
(Smiles, shrugs.)
Mmm.

Y. COURTENAY

They better be good. Angels is what you deserve. As sweet as you are with 'em.

JEWEL

They're *all* angels. At the school or at the church. Even the little devils got some angel in 'em.
(Looks at him pointedly, worriedly.)
You takin' care of yourself?

Y. COURTENAY

Awww, noooowww.

JEWEL

You not lettin' yourself go?

Y. COURTENAY

Let's not talk about me.

JEWEL

Let's talk about you...let's talk about you comin' home. And stayin' home. I know just about a dozen folks back home that'd get you some work. There's no real reason for—

Y. COURTENAY

You know there's a real reason. You know...I'll be goin' out—that's how it is. But never, just like a bad penny, you'll *never* be rid of me.

JEWEL

This livin' on the road—when you could have a nice home in Eatonville, where people live decent. Look at your eyes all sunk in. And your clothes just hangin' on you. *And where's your wedding band?* Sweet Jesus...

Y. COURTENAY

It's okay. I think it's in my horn case—I know it's in my horn case. I gotta take it off sometimes—I don't like anything on my fingers when I play. It's in with my horn.

JEWEL

You know, I almost believe that.

Y. COURTENAY

I swear it's the truth.

JEWEL

Well—even if it wasn't, why should it matter? Doesn't seem like I'm any kinda real wife to ya anyway. People back home wonderin' what kinda woman I am that—

Y. COURTENAY

We could talk about—something else.

JEWEL

You know, sometimes—I hate to say this—it's sin to say this—but there are times when it's even worse than when you went off to fight, 'cause I keep thinking—you didn't have any kinda choice about going to war, but you have a choice about bein' always on the road.

Y. COURTENAY

You really think I gotta choice in it?

JEWEL

I sometimes think that maybe...maybe since I haven't had babies, you don't think of me as a real wife. That maybe someday, when we have a baby, maybe then—

Y. COURTENAY

Oh, now, *no*. Babies don't have nothin' to do with it...baby.
          (He looks her straight in the eyes and smiles at her. She slowly returns the
          smile.)

JEWEL

I don't mean to go off on you. I just miss you so much...and I don't think you miss me the same way.

Y. COURTENAY

I miss you.

JEWEL

Then why keep all this up when I could be spoilin' you at home, 'stead of you sleepin' with bedbugs and—

Y. COURTENAY

I don't sleep with bedbugs.

JEWEL

You know what I mean. That place they've got you put up in.

Y. COURTENAY

You gonna change things for me, Mr. Adam Powell?

JEWEL

Don't get smart. I just think you deserve as good—even better than—the rest of those—

Y. COURTENAY

Now, let's not get into all that. I get things lined up just fine for myself—you don't need to worry about me. Mr. Stevens, he—

JEWEL

Keep talking.

Y. COURTENAY
(After a beat.)
You wanna know the truth? I wouldn't wanna stay around those guys anyway—it's good to get away from 'em. Wouldn't have it any other way.

JEWEL

Oh, now stop.

Y. COURTENAY

I mean it.

JEWEL
(Seriously.)
Stop.

Y. COURTENAY
(After a beat. Resigned.)
Well, baby: It's the way things are. And I can't change 'em.
(JEWEL turns away from him.)
Come on. Look, it's a *job*—a good job—somethin' to be thankful for. You ever seen this much back to back? More than I ever made back to back—and you're keeping it put up for us, huh?

JEWEL
You know I do. And I make plans for some of these days.

Y. COURTENAY
Yeah, that's worth somethin'. Thinkin' about the future.

JEWEL
Days pass, and I got plans and plans, on top of plans. But no you.

Y. COURTENAY
Ya gotta know that I've got plans, too...and they're all tied up with you. Gettin' in with a band that travels—this could be the beginning of a whole lotta sweetness.

JEWEL
Sweet for you.

Y. COURTENAY
I wouldn't want somethin' like this so much if it wasn't tied up with you, too. Money back to back, marked for you and for me, marked for *us.* And think: your folks and my folks—not gonna get anymore hasslin' from 'em 'bout me playin' for a livin' if this keeps up.

JEWEL
I'm glad good things are happening with your music, Court. It's just forever a hateful thing to, night and day, miss you so much.

Y. COURTENAY
I know, and I'll—*we'll* figure somethin' out. Maybe when you get holidays you can come out and travel with me proper.

JEWEL
I'm sure Mr. Stevens would be *delighted* to have your wife—

Y. COURTENAY
Oh, baby. Baby, it's the best I can do.

JEWEL
(Broken.)
The best you could do? The best you could do is to be my husband.

Y. COURTENAY
(Torn.)
Oh, baby, don't—baby, please.
(Softly, trying to comfort her.)
I wanna be good to you...but you...you knew when we got serious about each other, you knew how I felt about playing. You know.

JEWEL
I know.

Y. COURTENAY
You used to tell me...when you'd listen, you'd look at me and say things that made me feel like I could *have* or *do* anything with my music. Go anywhere with my music.

JEWEL
And you can...and you will...I just ...
(Resolved.)
And you should be able to. Anybody that can...create a *language* with that sad old pawn shop trombone...
(She holds his face in her hands, and quotes Langston Hughes.)
"I would liken you
To a night without stars
Were it not for your eyes.
I would liken you
To a sleep without dreams
Were it not for your songs."

Y. COURTENAY
(After a pause, taking it all in.)
You make my head spin. What is all that?

JEWEL
Langston Hughes. You should know Langston Hughes.

Y. COURTENAY
My schoolteacher. You got a head full of all kinds of stuff...so smart.

JEWEL
Not smart enough to keep you around.

Y. COURTENAY
Look...you can moan and groan all you like, but you can't deny—I love you and we belong to each other, for keeps. You don't believe me?

JEWEL
You know I believe you. I just wish...I wish I could—

Y. COURTENAY

What, baby?

JEWEL

I wish I could be your music. I wish I could be in your head and your heart and all through you—every second of the day—and say the beautiful things you make your music say. I wish I could dissolve and fill the air with the million things you make that horn of yours say.

Y. COURTENAY

Don't you know you do?
>   (He takes her hands.)
--As long as we're both under the same moon and stars.
>   (Wishes they were alone so he could kiss her. Touches her painted lips
>   with his index finger.)
Look at this...what do you need to paint yourself all up for?

JEWEL

For you.

Y. COURTENAY

This just messes up what's beautiful about you. What's this s'posed to be anyway? I've never seen *nobody* born with lips that color.

JEWEL

So now you tell me.
>   (She takes a handkerchief and small mirror out of her pocketbook and
>   begins to wipe away the lip rouge.)

Y. COURTENAY

Come on. Let me take you back over to the National. I gotta meet Jack over at The Arlington.

JEWEL

You can't sit still a minute, can you?

Y. COURTENAY

Gotta rehearse.

JEWEL

You two oughta be able to play symphonies by now.

Y. COURTENAY

Yeah, seems that way.

JEWEL

Now, you know I gotta be on the bus Wednesday morning. Maybe you can check into somebody taking me back to the Greyhound station.

Y. COURTENAY

I am, I am.

JEWEL

I don't feel right walkin' all by myself—

Y. COURTENAY

I'm takin' care of ya.

JEWEL

Um-hmm. And you're gone outta here on Wednesday, too? Late?

Y. COURTENAY

After the last set. Then all night on the road to New Orleans.

JEWEL

I wanna know all the details.

Y. COURTENAY

I got it, I got it all written down for you...somewhere. You need anything from over to the five and dime?

JEWEL
(Thinks, as she closes her pocketbook.)
No.

Y. COURTENAY

How about another ice cream?

JEWEL

No, I'm fine. That was just right—just enough.
(Looking into his eyes.)
And just enough's good enough, I suppose.
(He gently puts arm around her as they begin to walk away. Lights fade to black.)

ACT I
scene xi

(Lights up. COURTENAY's Miami Beach apartment, late 1988. The apartment is lit with a small amount of daylight coming in from the kitchen window. It can be seen that more items have been packed for the move, and any scattered trash has been taken away. The trunk is now fully visible. COURTENAY's trombone is out, resting on top of the kitchen table. A mellow jazz version of a Christmas standard emits from the radio—riddled with static.

After a moment, COURTENAY is heard unlocking the door to enter the apartment. As he opens the door, he turns on an interior light. He is seen wearing a light jacket, carrying something wrapped up in a sack from a hardware store. He removes a notice posted on the door—similar to the type of notice shown to him by EUGENIA in scene iii— makes a sour face and puts it in a coat pocket. He does not bother to read the notice in detail. After entering the apartment, he puts down the package and goes over to the radio. He turns the dial, trying to get better reception and in doing so, turns to the all news station.)

RADIO BROADCASTER 1
(A male voice with Cuban/Spanish dialect traces.)
...Super Bowl XXIII at Joe Robbie Stadium on January 22nd. Over 75,000 fans expected to be in attendance, a potential financial cash cow for Metro-Dade hotels, motels, restaurants, and retailers. Even without the opposing teams yet determined--

COURTENAY
(Turns off the radio, takes off his jacket and tosses it aside.)
75,000 fans...oh, yeahhhh...75,000 *drunks*...puking up and down Ocean Drive...cash cow— bullshit.

(COURTENAY picks up his trombone, runs through a scale, plays a quick jazz riff, then puts the horn away into its case. As he closes the case, he glares for a moment at the package. He takes his coat to the closet and puts it away. As he passes by the trunk, he looks it over momentarily. He goes to the kitchen, takes out a glass from a cabinet and pours himself some water from the tap. As he drinks the water, he stares across the room at the package and the trunk. He pauses and sets the glass of water down and goes and picks up the package. He turns it over in his hands as he moves to the trunk. He stares at the trunk and slowly crouches before it. He sets the package aside. He reaches out and touches the trunk, running his fingers over the découpage work, stopping to contemplate some of the travel related stickers covering it, and delicately touching the cracked/worn/weathered places on its surface. Carefully, he takes the rusted lock in hand and rattles it. He drops it, slowly rubs his rust covered fingertips together, and then rises and moves away from the trunk. He paces within the room, then _suddenly_ turns, and—in _one_ swift uniform movement—grabs the package, tears it open revealing an iron crowbar, and rips the lock from the trunk. He drops the crowbar and glares at the trunk. As he slowly begins to kneel before the trunk, a knock is heard at the door. He lets the knock repeat. He rises and begins to move to the door—stopping, just briefly, to put everything about the trunk into the back of his mind. He answers the door. A white man in his mid-sixties is seen in COURTENAY's doorway. The man's hair is silver and slate, and he wears a moustache. He is dressed in a cheap, well-worn sportscoat, paired with trousers and tie. He wears an old homberg or fedora. He grips a piece of paper with information.)

COURTENAY

Yes?

(The man does not speak. He removes his hat and looks at COURTENAY with wide eyes.)

Well? What is it that—

(COURTENAY begins to wonder/realize.)

—I can..._what_...

JACK

(Not _completely_ certain that he is indeed in the company of COURTENAY.)

Looking for Courtenay Dees.

(A pause. COURTENAY is momentarily speechless.)

Jack Fornett...looking for—Courtenay Dees.

COURTENAY

(Full realization/comprehension sweeps over him.)

I'd say you've got his full attention.

(Fade to black.)

End of ACT I

ACT II
scene i

>(Lights up. COURTENAY's Miami Beach apartment, late 1988. The set is unchanged from the final scene of Act I. COURTENAY and JACK are in the kitchen area; JACK is seated at the table while COURTENAY is at the kitchen counter.)

COURTENAY
That must be somethin'...to have somebody wanna see your face that bad.

JACK
I think stalking's what they call it. I hope he didn't make any trouble for you. I know there's somethin' about him meanin' well. He went on about...well, he was surprised to hear that you and I hadn't kept in touch.
>(Changes the topic.)

I guess, from all he's said, his mother must have really built us up.
>(Pause. Though JACK seems easygoing enough, as if he is simply making a run of the mill visit, he has an undercurrent of unease.)

COURTENAY
He told me after his father died in '78—I mean, after Lola Rae's husband died in—

JACK
I know what you mean.

COURTENAY
And that right about after that, she started up talkin' ...and that was the first he knew. Of you.

JACK
>(Quietly, confirming.)

Yeah.

COURTENAY
First he ever knew. And when she started up, she talked like, like it was yesterday. And she made it seem like we'd all been some kinda close.

JACK
We were—to her.
>(A pause.)

Brings back a whole lot, doesn't it?

COURTENAY
I should say it does. It brought you around.

                              JACK
So when did you hear from him?

                            COURTENAY
Ohhhh, 'round a week ago.

                              JACK
Yeah...it wasn't too long after that he got in touch with me. I thought it was some kinda crazy joke at first. He called up askin' for me, then mentioned her name—*did I remember*...and how she died 'bout a year ago. How he just felt the need to somehow reconcile.
                    (A little lost for a moment.)
I was just sittin' there...watchin' the TV and then all of a sudden...I was talking to my son.

                            COURTENAY
Where's there?

                              JACK
Pompano Beach.

                            COURTENAY
You dog. You're up in Pompano?

                              JACK
I'm up in Pompano.

                            COURTENAY
How long?

                              JACK
Little over a year. Used to get away to South Florida every chance I could. Now it's home, my home.

                            COURTENAY
So, Mr. Pompano Beach...you make yourself a habit of just showin' up at people's doors after near about forty years?

                              JACK
I called, I let it ring. Tried to give you fair notice. You out a lot or somethin'?

                            COURTENAY
Sometimes I just don't like to pick up.

                              JACK
I thought: I'm thinkin' 'bout goin' down to South Beach to see somebody who might not even...but he said you two spoke for quite a while, and he said why not go, *why not?* Said he felt

JACK cont'd

the address was good, so I took it down. I thought, hell, if I get down there and worse comes to worst, I'll just go suck down some brews on the beach.

COURTENAY

So this stalking thing runs in the family for ya.

JACK
(Wistfully.)
Humph. *Family*. I got family.
(After a pause.)
You know, he thought for sure that—I mean, he was genuinely surprised we hadn't kept up with each other. And he was just *stupified* about us *both* bein' in Florida, wantin' to know if I was *sure* I hadn't seen or heard of ya.

COURTENAY

What's that s'posed to mean?

JACK

Hell if I know. You say, "I gotta condo in Pompano..." and somebody says, "South Florida? Maybe you know..." What the hell is that?

COURTENAY

Don't ask me.

JACK

Like they're thinkin' there's just six people out here and we're all keepin' tabs on each other.

COURTENAY

Yeahhhh.

JACK

Yeahhhh. He just thought it was so interestin' that we *both* ended up in South Florida.
(Voice trails off.)

COURTENAY

There's nothin' to us both bein'...

JACK

Well...

COURTENAY

Nothin' real surprising about a couple of old men wantin' their own time in the sun. Nothin' to us both bein'—

JACK

Well. Might be.

COURTENAY

I don't think so. I grew up in Orange County, in Eatonville, and—

JACK
(Quietly.)

I know.

COURTENAY

--just decided to go home. Ended up that Eatonville had too many memories. So I came down here. During on-season, you can put some pretty good work together.

JACK
(Sees the trombone case and links it with what COURTENAY has just said.)

You still play?

COURTENAY

I still breathe, too.
(JACK is quiet and fixed on the trombone case. After a beat.)
What? You don't play?

JACK

Last gig: a week at the Glen Island Casino in New Rochelle, 1951—just as the gilt was fading from the lily. I sat in for—I covered for a guy who had to go home 'cause his wife dropped a litter. He already had snapshots...snapshots when he got back.
(His voice trails off weakly.)

COURTENAY
(Impressed.)

Glen Island Casino.

JACK

Last hurrah. After that, I sold the horn and went back to Kansas City. My Granddad got me back on the railroad.

COURTENAY

What?

JACK

Kansas City Southern, K.C.S., 36 years of service. That's how I come to retire—with a full pension. Good benefits, good pay—got health, got dental.
(JACK shows off his teeth with a weird smile.)
They took good care of me. Still do. Just retired summer of last year.

COURTENAY

I'm not following you here.

JACK

Not following what?

COURTENAY

You stopped playin' in '51?

JACK

Uhm-hmm.

COURTENAY

You sold your horn?

JACK

I worked for the railroad during the war and there was a good place for me back there. I knew I could have something, have myself a life, and a lot less...I don't know. The music ended up bein' all tied into a buncha baggage for me. I got rid of a whole lotta baggage when I sold that horn.

COURTENAY

Woulda never, never guessed that.

JACK

So you've kept with it?

COURTENAY

I woulda never guessed, Jack, that you'd...*never guessed that.*

JACK

It just wasn't...
(Sighs.)
With the railroad, I knew I was gonna have somethin' definite that gave back to me. I worked up and through the ranks—worked up to and retired as a conductor. I had myself something real there, something to count on. As long as I gave K.C.S. a little of me, I got back. No regrets there. I got a condo in Pompano.
(Repeating COURTENAY.)
My place in the sun. I've retired to South Florida like a million other people, who've worked hard all their lives and now are ready just to enjoy the salt breeze, the warmth on their backs. Like a million other people who wanted *somethin'*...so did I. And the music...
                    (His voice trails off. Very soft and ethereal sounding, a few bars of
                    Big Band inspired clarinet and trombone music are heard. The
                    music is a memory, which plays softly under the continuing
                    dialogue.)

COURTENAY
(After a pause.)
Would've never guessed.

JACK

Like I said, I had a lotta baggage with the music. Too much.

> (The two men become lost in thoughts of the past for a moment. With lights remaining full up on JACK and COURTENAY, lights slowly come up on a second acting area, to reveal YOUNG JACK and YOUNG COURTENAY on their instruments. The young men are half in shadow, as if held in a clouded memory. A black and white slide image of the interior of a modest recording studio, 1948, acts as backdrop for the young musicians. As the song wraps, YOUNG JACK looks off to where the recording engineer is assumed to be, and waits for a signal indicating that recording is complete. YOUNG JACK speaks after he is "given" the signal.)

Y. JACK

He got it.

Y. COURTENAY

That's fine.

Y. JACK

Noooo, not so fine...I'm gonna see if we can try it one more time.

Y. COURTENAY

The sound was good, Jack. Let's give it a listen.

Y. JACK

I don't wanna listen to crap.

Y. COURTENAY

Aw, nooowww.

Y. JACK

Come on, we might as well do it right. I'll go talk to him—I'll tell him we just needed to settle in--and this time, don't go off so much.

Y. COURTENAY

What are you talking about? It was *good*. It was real good. There's no reason to—

Y. JACK

Don't go and get lazy on me. It'll take the guy maybe five or ten to set it up again. Take yourself a breather if ya gotta, and think about—

Y. COURTENAY

Hold it. If you're so hot to cut it again, we better just see about tomorrow.

Y. JACK

What?

Y. COURTENAY

We gotta get outta Little Rock right now if we're gonna be back in Hot Springs for rehearsal. Tiny's got new arrangements we gotta learn before our gig in the Big Easy. If we're gonna be playin' the Monteleone, Jack, we gotta--

Y. JACK

I'm not thinkin' about Tiny or N'awlins or the goddamn Monteleone right now. I wanna get this cut and *right,* and there's no tomorrow. I swung us time in here for *today.*

Y. COURTENAY

This record cutting thing's swell and all, but man, what's some vanity recordin' gonna do for us if we go and get under Tiny's skin? Gotta think about where our pay's comin' from.

Y. JACK

Wellll, you're just full of advice, ain't ya? Now listen, don't you go throwin' orders around here—you got a mouth, and it's gonna get you in trouble. Maybe *you* have to step-n-fetchit for the Tiny Stevens Orchestra but *I* don't.

Y. COURTENAY
(Backs away and begins to pace like an animal in a cage.)
Oh, nooowww.

Y. JACK

And what in the hell do ya mean saying—*vanity recordin'?* Where'd you get that? This is gonna be our calling card...oh, why do I hafta explain somethin' to a lazy...Christ.

Y. COURTENAY

I can't stay here, Jack.

Y. JACK

Oh, really? Well, looks like ya just might hafta to reconsider, 'cause if you don't, you're walkin' boy, and you sure as hell won't be back in time to kiss Tiny's ass if you're walkin'.

Y. COURTENAY
(Using every fiber of his being to control himself. Not facing Y. JACK.
Calmly, measuredly, *almost* softly.)
We cut our calling card. It's a *good* sound. Now we pick it up and we get outta here. There's no bein' some big name in one afternoon.

Y. JACK
(JACK begins to react physically, allowing pent up energy to escape
through gesture and breathing.)
You just don't get it do you? We're not some guys workin' on a factory line or diggin' ditches

Y. JACK cont'd

or—we got some kinda somethin' that can fit into the future, somethin' important here. Screw Tiny, screw whoever tries to get in our way.

Y. COURTENAY

Jack, maybe you can talk your way outta trouble with Tiny, but I can't. I don't want to lose this gig, man. For the first time, ever, I'm able to send money home to my wife, dependable-like--

Y. JACK

Dependable? Maybe you *oughta* be out diggin' ditches for your wife if dependable's all you need. Look: I'll play the heavy when we get back to The Arlington if that's what it takes. Don't worry about your chickenshit ass gettin' canned—I'll smooth it over, I'll tell the man whatever the hell he wants to hear. We're makin' *our* music today, Court—ya understand? And I'm not lettin' Tiny, Harry Truman, or even *you* get in the way of it.

> (Y. COURTENAY stands in the silence. as Y. JACK exits. The lights fade to black in the recording studio/second acting area. In the apartment, in silence, COURTENAY pours coffee for JACK.)

JACK

So-uh...you and your wife...did you two last?

COURTENAY

Jewel died in '55, cancer.

JACK

I'm sorry.

COURTENAY

I was in Eatonville with her for a while when she got real bad with it. After she died, I let our house go, then I stayed on the road back to back.

JACK

No children?

COURTENAY

Never did have children.

JACK

Maybe you can count yourself lucky.

COURTENAY

> (Looks away from JACK, purposefully does not respond to the comment.)

You-uh...you ever settle? Get married and settled?

JACK

Never got married and never settled down. Mighta gotten married, but I don't imagine it woulda ever settled me down. I've always had somethin' goin'. The guys at K.C.S. used to say...
                    (Smiles, shrugs.)
I gave the guys things to talk about.

COURTENAY

Can I ask ya...

JACK

Ask me.

COURTENAY

Lola Rae...you two ever had any kinda—you two spoke, or anything, after the last time you saw each other?

JACK

The call from William was the first I'd even heard her name since after...after we spoke last in New Orleans. When the band was playin' in New Orleans, I don't know if you recall—she came into town. Found me in Jackson Square.
                    (His voice trails off.)

COURTENAY

                    (Quietly.)
I know, Jack. Remember?

                    (There is a pause. JACK suddenly begins to move about the room, as
                    if wants to shakes something off.)

JACK

He--William...he wants me to spend some time with him and his family, over the holidays. Christmas through New Year's. I've gone and said yes. I mean, I've spent dozens of Christmases alone. Granddad's long gone, mother's gone, never wasted the effort collectin' myself any distant relatives. Things are quiet. So why not go see him? *Why not?*

COURTENAY

Well, nice for some, but I'd have reservations 'bout pickin' up to spend Christmas with a strange man who wanted to call me Daddy.

JACK

Awwww, don't you watch TV? People do this all the time nowadays. You can just be sittin' or standin' *anywhere*, and suddenly you find out you got a child, or a half dozen brothers and sisters, unclaimed wealth with the treasury...*it's the eighties.* This is all perfectly natural. Keep up with the times, man.

COURTENAY

But is this somethin' you really want?

JACK

This guy, this William...he doesn't sound half bad. He says he's got a lake house he goes to for the weekends.

COURTENAY

I'm sure that makes him a real fine person.

JACK

He sounds okay. He works for Frito-Lay—*corporate*—in Dallas. That's gotta be a good job. Some kinda job with an office. Benefits.

COURTENAY

Someday he might have a condo in Pompano.

JACK

Exactly. And he's got a wife and two children. Wife doesn't even have to work—she does some kinda little volunteer thing or somethin'. I could just walk right in and play old Santa Claus for all of 'em.
                    (After a beat, thoughtfully.)
I can see how it all goes.

COURTENAY

He doesn't have any bitterness, or what have you?

JACK

What would he have to be bitter about? He had a mother *and* father to raise him. It just wasn't ever meant to be with me and Lola Rae. It just wasn't part of this lifetime, not in the cards.
                    (A pause. Reflectively.)
You know...I don't know what she told him, but he thinks I musta been somethin'. And it—you know, it blew him away when I said I hadn't played in years. It seemed like, it seemed as if she'd built me up as some kinda...isn't that odd—truly *odd?* If anybody would've ever asked, I'da said she'd had me shot before kind words.

COURTENAY

And I woulda counted on it.

JACK

But he talked, he talked like...
                    (Shakes his head, thoughtfully.
                    Starts up again.)
Said he'd been through a private detective, libraries, placed ads, calls to all kinds of people, false leads...time, effort and *money*...on wantin' to hear my voice, see my face.

COURTENAY

Hope he's not disappointed.

JACK

Then he got 'round to talkin' 'bout you, and he mentioned he had your number. I asked him to pass it on—and here I am.

COURTENAY

You come down here special just for me?

JACK

Awwww, South Beach ain't so hard on the eyes. I may stay a coupla days.

COURTENAY

You gonna be flyin' out to Texas?

JACK

I should. Looks like a drive would take near to three days. But I got a lotta thinkin' to do and a drive just might give me a chance to do my thinkin'.

COURTENAY

Sometimes thinkin' for...three straight days...can give you some kinda headache.

JACK

Maybe.
                    (A pause. He is near the trombone case. He turns to COURTENAY.)
So you've been playin' all these years?

COURTENAY

That's what I do, Jack.

JACK

You had a good life after Tiny Stevens?

COURTENAY

I made my own way fine after Tiny Stevens. You name it. Combos, clubs, sometimes sat in with bands that needed somebody in a temporary way—but nothin', *nothin'* more that'd tie me down.
                    (Staring JACK down.)
Had a real bad taste left with me after Tiny Stevens, about that kinda work..."dependable" work.

JACK

Um-hm.

COURTENAY

Played solo in jobs as they came—and now as they come. Sometimes I take the bus to Dadeland or Kendall—I can play a whole day in and outta retirement homes that set me up.

JACK

You just got the world by its ear.

COURTENAY

I play for whoever can find enjoyment in it, and for whoever can find some cash to spare. I play to get just enough of what it takes to keep a person decent.
(They connect for a moment.)
I never been interested in bein' some kinda name, Jack.
(There is a brief moment in which COURTENAY's comment appears to just slide by JACK. Then, just as briefly, JACK connects with the comment and something of a wince is seen on his face. He attempts to recover.)

JACK

Well, I s'pose I've inflicted myself on you long enough. Just thought it'd be good to-uh...

COURTENAY

Yeah.

JACK

Uhm-hmm. I gotta reservation over at the Fontainebleau.

COURTENAY

Good for you.

JACK

Gotta get myself checked in. Then maybe get out and do a little shoppin'. Get myself some South Beach threads, somethin' to make 'em take notice in Big D.

COURTENAY

(Good naturedly.)
Ya better do somethin'. Looks like ya been tradin' at the old man's store.

JACK

(With a wink and a smile.)
What? These are my good impression clothes.

COURTENAY

Just for me? Shouldn't have bothered. I think I got my impression of you a long time ago, Jack Fornett.

JACK

(Humbly, quietly.)
I know...I know.
(After a beat, moving on.)
Soooo, you got plans for Christmas?

                    COURTENAY
Waitin' for Christmas to make plans for me this year.

                    JACK
Maybe I'll give ya a call again, before I leave town.

                    COURTENAY
Maybe I'll feel like pickin' up.

                    JACK
It's been good to talk.

                    COURTENAY
It's been fine.

                    JACK
         (At the door, trying to avoid any kind of awkward goodbye.)
You went and got fat.

                    COURTENAY
You went and got old.

                    JACK
Aaaaaaa...*so what.*
         (Hesitantly.)
I'll-uh...I'll see ya, Court.

                    COURTENAY
Yeah, Jack.

         (The two men stand looking at one another—neither extending a
         hand nor making any movement to connect in any physical way.)

                    JACK
I'll see you around.

         (COURTENAY watches JACK leave and move down the corridor.
         COURTENAY then, slowly and with effort, closes the door. He turns and
         faces the living area of the apartment, appearing to be lost in a jumble of
         thoughts. His eyes come to rest on the crowbar and trunk. Fade to black.)

ACT II
scene ii

(Lights up. 1948. A slide projection reflects a piece of original music, clearly titled, "One Beautiful Thing to Remember." The music is composed in pencil, with the notes appearing to have been hurriedly "flung" onto the hand drawn staffs. This slide projection will serve as the backdrop for two separate and distinct acting areas, side by side in front of the projection, separated only by lighting effects. The content of each room/acting area is meant to simply *suggest* the accommodations.

The first acting area reflects the contents of a modest room at Hot Springs' National Bath House/Hotel. The room is taken by YOUNG COURTENAY and, for the time being, JEWEL. The room is furnished with a bed, a chair, and a side table. The furniture is structurally sound, but well-worn and of a simple, almost nondescript design. The trombone case rests against the side table. An old suitcase, locks broken and held shut by a leather belt, rests against the side of the bed. The trunk seen in COURTENAY's Miami apartment is on the floor at the foot of the bed, in, of course, newer condition with less découpage and fewer travel related stickers.

The second acting area reflects the contents of a small room at the Arlington Hotel, taken by YOUNG JACK. The bed, chair, and small desk reflect an art deco influence and each piece is in good condition. The clarinet case is open and empty, and rests on the small desk.

Lights come up slowly on the first acting area: JEWEL is seen, sitting in the chair, watching YOUNG COURTENAY nap. Lights then rise on the second acting area; YOUNG JACK has just completed playing his song.)

LOLA RAE
I've got it, I got it—I know what you can call it!
(Sings/speaks in a rhythmic pattern.)
One beautiful thing to remember, my love. I know, I know, I can't sing.

Y. JACK

You gettin' creative on me here?

LOLA RAE

That's what I hear—those words. They're right in there. What do you think? It fits, huh?

Y. JACK

Well, it's not really supposed to have lyrics...it's an instrumental.
>   (In the first acting area, as dialogue in the second area continues, JEWEL
>   rises from the chair and quietly goes to the trunk.)

LOLA RAE

But it's gotta have a name.

Y. JACK

Well—yeah.

LOLA RAE

Well, that's its name—*title*. It's right there.
>   (Speaks slowly and simply in a rhythmic pattern.)

One beautiful thing to remember, my love.
>   (JEWEL takes a record out of the trunk.)

It fits so perfectly—you think? Can you see how it would fit? I think…it would fit. Do you
think?

>   (JEWEL holds the record up to the light and studies the grooves, runs her
>   fingers over the grooves. She hums softly to herself.)

Y. JACK

You wanna name the song?

LOLA RAE

You'd let me name the song?

Y. JACK

Name the song.
>   (Speaking/singing to the rhythm, awkwardly to remember what she said:)

One big thing you can't forget—

LOLA RAE

Noooo—*one beautiful thing to remember*. And there's a *my love* in there, too, but that'd
probably make it too long.

Y. JACK

One beautiful thing to remember…
>   (Looking her in the eyes.)

my love.

LOLA RAE

Yeah. Yeah.

(Happy.)

You like it?

Y. JACK

Yeah—sure—it's great.

LOLA RAE

You think you'll really keep it?

Y. JACK

Why not? It's right. It's…good.

LOLA RAE

So—that's it. I named the song. I named your big song. I think I love that.

Y. JACK

Little Miss Arkansas named the song.

LOLA RAE

I named the song.

(In the first acting area, Y. COURTENAY begins to wake. He sees JEWEL with the record.)

Y. COURTENAY

What are you up to?

JEWEL

Wishing I could hear this.

Y. COURTENAY

I'll play it for you on my horn whenever—you just ask.

JEWEL

No, there's something special about it being right on a record.

Y. COURTENAY

It's just a vanity record—anybody can cut one. It's not like—

JEWEL

Shut your mouth, I love it. As soon as I'm back home I'm going over to Leona's. She's got a record player and I'm gonna play it 'til there's not a note left on it.

Y. COURTENAY

And what'll Leona think of that?

JEWEL
(Threateningly.)

She'll like it.

Y. COURTENAY
(Shakes his head, pulls her to him.)

You.

(She teasingly breaks away from him and goes to the trunk.)

JEWEL

Here...you wear a fresh shirt tonight.
(She takes a white, crisply starched, button down shirt from the trunk.)

Y. COURTENAY

You brought me a new shirt?

JEWEL

I brought you two. *And* I've decided...I want you to keep the trunk. I want you to have enough room for everything you need when you're travelling.

Y. COURTENAY

Your trunk?

JEWEL

You should have it.

Y. COURTENAY

It's yours...it's got all those paper stickers on it I sent back to you, special. It's *your* trunk.

JEWEL

You need it. You're the one lives on the road.

Y. COURTENAY

Baby, I can't be haulin' that trunk around with me everywhere.

JEWEL
(Points at his sad old suitcase.)
Look what you're living out of, Courtenay. That's sad.

Y. COURTENAY

I travel light.

JEWEL

None of your things can stay any kind of respectable in that. Why do you wanna carry that? You gotta show people you got some pride. You don't want—

Y. COURTENAY
(Obligingly.)
Okay, okay, I'll take the trunk. If it'll make you happy.

JEWEL·
I can't watch out for you and take care of you like a wife should. But this trunk—you can lock your things in it, and keep your things safe, under lock and key, and--

Y. COURTENAY
I'm takin' it. I might break my back hauling it all over, but...come here, you.
            (Y. COURTENAY grabs JEWEL for a quick kiss. After a pause, she
            tenderly kisses him back. In the second acting area, Y. JACK winds down
            his playing. Y. COURTENAY and JEWEL cuddle as dialogue in the
            second acting area progresses.)

LOLA RAE
I can't wait to tell my friends—when you're fabulously famous—that I got to name the song.

Y. JACK
You'll be the toast of Hot Springs, my dear.

LOLA RAE
Well, actually, most of my friends—most of the people I *really* know—are up East.

Y. JACK
East?

LOLA RAE
We moved to Arkansas when I was sixteen, from Pennsylvania, after my Daddy died. My Momma's got family here.

Y. JACK
So you're not really Little Miss Arkansas, Queen of Hot Springs?

LOLA RAE
I was born in Moon Run, Pennsylvania.

Y. JACK
I think I'm disappointed.

LOLA RAE
Why? Don't be. Sometimes I'm glad this place isn't my real hometown.

Y. JACK
It's not that bad.

LOLA RAE

It *can* be bad. The way that people...sometimes I think there's something around here that brings out a badness in people. Like the other day, when you and Courtenay were...you sounded for a second like the way some of the...I thought you—

Y. JACK

Thought I *what?* You think too much.

LOLA RAE

Yeah. I guess so. I—well, I'm just glad that...I'm glad this isn't *home* home. I wanna move back up East someday. Things aren't perfect anywhere, but at least back home—

Y. JACK

Shhhh. You're wrinkling up your forehead. Too much thinkin'. Remember—simple.
(Y. JACK kisses her softly, then more passionately.)

LOLA RAE

You know, I should go. I really should. I just wanted to—

Y. JACK

Just wanted to what?

LOLA RAE

To hear your song, and talk, and—

Y. JACK

You could hear my song and talk to me anywhere, Lola Rae.

LOLA RAE

I know. But I...

Y. JACK

But you what?

LOLA RAE

I...

Y. JACK

Uhm-hmm?

LOLA RAE

I know what you mean, but I—

Y. JACK

You can't, you don't want to, I know. I'm just foolin' around.

LOLA RAE

It's not that I can't. It's not that I don't want to. I'd just like to know, to...you remember, you said about trusting a musician?

Y. JACK

That you can't.

LOLA RAE
(Seriously, after a beat.)
I think I'd like to be able to trust you, Jack.

Y. JACK

Trust me about what? Oh, Lola Rae.

LOLA RAE

That you'd...

Y. JACK

That I'd what?

LOLA RAE

That you'd never forget me. That I'd always be in your head, Little Miss Arkansas from Pennsylvania...if you and I, if we...
> (Y. JACK studies her for a moment, and then turns away, realizing she is quite serious. As dialogue in the first acting area begins again, Y. JACK begins to take his clarinet apart and return it to its case. LOLA RAE watches him quietly.)

JEWEL

So am I walkin' or ridin' to the bus station tomorrow?

Y. COURTENAY

You're ridin'. In style. A black Packard. Jack'll be drivin'. It's Tiny's, Tiny's lettin' us use his car.

JEWEL

Thank the Lord. I got a scare walkin' in. This is not the kinda place for—

Y. COURTENAY

What kinda scare? What're you talkin' about?

JEWEL

It was nothin'. There was this truck with some young men.

Y. COURTENAY

White men.

JEWEL

They tried running me off the road down into a creek. But then they got too smart for themselves and almost spun out.

Y. COURTENAY
(Beginning to grow visibly angry.)
Why didn't you tell me about this?

JEWEL

'Cause...well, look at you...*see?*

Y. COURTENAY

Look at me *what?*

JEWEL

You're breathin' and your eyes are all wild.

Y. COURTENAY

They tried to run you over.

JEWEL

They wanted to scare me.

Y. COURTENAY
They coulda done worse than just scare. You know. *My God.*

JEWEL

Nooowww. You got me a ride for tomorrow, things are okay. Don't go and mess up this last little bit of time we got before you hafta get back to The Arlington.

Y. COURTENAY

God...*God bless...*

JEWEL

Come on.
(Trying to change the subject.)
Come on, why don't you...you know tonight, why don't I go over with you? I can be real quiet, back out of the way, in *nobody's* way, just for this last night to hear you.

Y. COURTENAY
(Still visibly upset, pacing.)
I'd...I really think it'd be best if ya—

JEWEL

Ohhhh, just sit still for a minute—just—oh, what am I thinkin'? You can't sit still, you couldn't even if you wanted. But just look at me, and quit starin' out all wild. Just stop.

Y. COURTENAY
(He begins to try to calm himself.)

Okay. Okay.

(She touches him, and calms him further. She rubs his shoulders.)

JEWEL

So you're gonna take me with you tonight, to hear the—

Y. COURTENAY

You heard us yesterday afternoon. It's still the same.

JEWEL

I'd like to hear you-all play your show.

Y. COURTENAY

It's the same as practice.

JEWEL

It'd be something I'd like.

Y. COURTENAY

I'd--I'd just rather you...
(He looks at her helplessly.)

JEWEL

I see. That's the way with them, huh? I thought—*I don't know why*—but I thought it was different.

Y. COURTENAY

Most of the guys are fine, Tiny can be fine, it's just sometimes...

JEWEL

It's Jack, isn't it? I was barely able to say "good to meet you" before you tore me away from him. And the mood you're in after you two rehearse. What are you hidin', Court? He's not your boss. What's he got over you that—

Y. COURTENAY

I'm not hidin' anything. He just—he's—he wants us to make good, he wants us to make something good for ourselves. But he can be hard to take, *sometimes*, and I don't want him bein' hard to take around you. Like the record. We cut this—when you listen you'll understand. It's good. It is *good*. But after three different takes, he *still* wasn't satisfied and he walked right out of the session without even botherin' to pick it up. Some guy came runnin' out with it and I took it. He wouldn't. He's got himself so tied up in what he *thinks* he needs that sometimes...

JEWEL

If he's so hard to take, what exactly is it that he's dishin' out?
(Y. COURTENAY looks away.)

JEWEL cont'd

If you're not gettin' treated right by *any* of these people, Court—it doesn't matter about how much you're gettin' back to back, 'cause it probably isn't half of what—

Y. COURTENAY

It still's—

JEWEL

No.

Y. COURTENAY

Jewel.

JEWEL

No, you listen—

Y. COURTENAY

Jewel, *please.*

(Feeling more frustration than he can deal with, Y. COURTENAY sits down and faces away from JEWEL. At this point, in the second acting area, LOLA RAE begins to speak.)

LOLA RAE

I look at you Jack—and maybe it's that I wish that *I* had a beautiful song, and that I went all over to interesting places, and that I made music that people could fall in love to...with their heads full of half-real things that people think about when they're in love. That's what you do. It's more than just playing in a band. It's about making a *world* where people can have some happiness for a little while.

Y. JACK

(Turning to face her.)

You're too good be true.

LOLA RAE

You're...oh, I don't know what you are.

Y. JACK

I'm not Billy Odell Davies.

LOLA RAE

I guess maybe that's *it.*

Y. JACK

(Extremely serious, but gentle.)

I'm here today and gone tomorrow, and I know you need something more than that. I can't cheat you of your future. If I'd just been here for a night, and you were just some kinda...

LOLA RAE

I know that after you're gone, I'll still hear your song in my head. I know the day that I marry—and I know, *he* is the man that I'll marry—I'll still hear your song in my head.

Y. JACK

So maybe you shouldn't be comin' up to my room.

(LOLA RAE watches as Y. JACK turns away from her. Dialogue begins again in the first acting area.)

JEWEL

If you're out there on the road gettin' beaten down by...Court, I have enough trouble sleepin' without knowin' that you're—

Y. COURTENAY

I'm here for the same reasons that've ever taken me anywhere: to a see little of this world while I'm in it and to play as much I possibly can. And if what makes that good ever changes, then I'll know it's time to move on. As long as the music's good, I can stay, with whatever it is, wherever it is. You see? And now, for the first time, I found somethin' where I can do my music *and* do right by you, too—see? You know what I've been sendin' you is more than—

JEWEL

I can do fine—

Y. COURTENAY

I just want to—

JEWEL

(Forcefully.)

No, *listen* to me. I can't tell you who you can make your music with—but I *can* say this: I make enough to make my way, Court. Don't you for a second take any kind of ill treatment for my sake over money.

Y. COURTENAY

I don't take anything I can't—

JEWEL

Don't you *dare* let them treat you with *nothing* but respect, 'cause I can't—I can't deal with you not taking care of yourself. You hear me?

Y. COURTENAY

(Trying to calm/comfort her.)

Just...you just...

JEWEL

Do you hear me???

(The dialogue in the second acting area begins again, as Y. COURTENAY continues to comfort JEWEL.)

Y. JACK

We had a nice two weeks, huh? Somethin' we can both think about. Now things just move on, Lola Rae. That's all there is to it. You don't want—
(At this point, the dialogue between the two acting areas begins to overlap.)

LOLA RAE

I want to know, if I could...

JEWEL

I know...

LOLA RAE

If I could trust you...

JEWEL

That no matter where you go I can trust you. I don't worry about that.

Y. JACK

What do you need to trust me about?

Y. COURTENAY

You don't worry about that.

LOLA RAE

That you won't forget me...

JEWEL

I *know*...that you carry me in your head. And that's what gets me by.

LOLA RAE

'Cause if I knew that...

JEWEL

I could get through anything, even your death someday, God forbid it, just knowin' that you and I...we're together.

LOLA RAE

If I knew...

JEWEL

But I gotta know you don't ever cheat yourself. I know you'd never cheat me, but I also gotta know that you *don't cheat yourself.* That you never forget your self-respect.

LOLA RAE

–that you'd never forget me, I would stay. Because I can. And I because I want to.

JEWEL

And it doesn't matter where you chase your music to, I can deal with you chasin' your dreams. You see? I just need one thing to get me by...

LOLA RAE

To have one beautiful thing to remember after your music is gone.

JEWEL

I want to know that *you* treat *you* right.

LOLA RAE

I want to belong to you, just for a little while.

JEWEL
(Beginning to tremble.)

I gotta know that you respect yourself as much as you respect you music.

LOLA RAE

Do you understand?

JEWEL

Understand, Court?

> (As Y. COURTENAY stands frozen, almost stunned by his wife's show of emotion and zeal, Y. JACK takes LOLA RAE's face in his hands and pulls her to him.)

LOLA RAE

I just...

> (JACK kisses her deeply. The lights on the second acting area begin to fade to black. The lights on the first acting area linger a little longer on JEWEL and Y. COURTENAY.)

JEWEL
(Losing her composure.)

Gotta know...that you never let them cheat you of *you*...
> (JEWEL lets go a choked sob.)
...of who you are...*I gotta know.*
> (Y. COURTENAY pulls JEWEL closely to him and she clings tightly. The lights in the first acting area fade to black.)

ACT II
scene iii

(Lights up. COURTENAY's Miami Beach apartment, late 1988. The trunk is opened, with various keepsake items—dating from the 40s and early 50s—removed from it and placed nearby. The items include the vanity record, a scrapbook, Eatonville newspapers, a book of Langston Hughes poetry published in the 40s, an inexpensive jewelry box, the hat with the bird of paradise, a marriage certificate, and a slightly yellowed wedding dress— small and modest and folded over so that it is barely discernable as a wedding dress. A knock is heard at the front door. After a moment another knock is heard—and then EUGENIA's voice.)

EUGENIA
(Offstage.)

This is wearin' me down, Court. It's not like you got more than five steps in any direction to get to the door. This is showin' a lack of respect, that's all it comes down to. R-E-S-P-E-C-T.
(She rattles the doorknob.)
I got some interestin' news.
(Rattles the knob again.)
Court, if you want me to go away and leave you be, just give two good raps on the wall and I'll leave you in peace.
(Quiet. Then briskly.)
Okay, I'm comin' in.

(EUGENIA lets herself in and sees that no one is there. She grimaces, and starts leave—then notices the keepsakes removed from the trunk.)
Well, my God...you finally let all the skeletons out.
(She starts to leave again, but then turns back to survey the keepsakes, leaving the door ajar. She kneels and picks up the hat with the bird of paradise and looks it over for a moment. She puts it down and picks up an old Eatonville, Florida, newspaper—late '40s or early '50s. COURTENAY arrives at the front door, peeks in, and then enters—not pleased to find that EUGENIA has entered on her own. He carries a large brown paper sack from a Publix grocery store, with the top of the bag folded over.)

COURTENAY

What can I do for you, Eugenia?

EUGENIA

I see you got your trunk opened up.

COURTENAY

Yes.

EUGENIA

I just walked in, haven't been here but just two shakes.

COURTENAY

Fine.

(COURTENAY goes and puts the grocery sack on top of the refrigerator.)

EUGENIA

I mean, I knocked—I knocked first—but then I thought that maybe you...
(Feels his cold reception.)
Oh, now, Court. I wasn't comin' in here for any ill intent, I...

COURTENAY

You do whatever you like. You're the property manager.

EUGENIA

(After a beat.)
I was just thinkin' that maybe you ...ohhhh...I suppose maybe I *wasn't* thinkin'.
(Pause. Silence.)
I wanted to tell you...I have some news, and I was just so determined to tell you that I...

COURTENAY

(Still cool.)
I got the notice on the door—'bout the move-out, just like you said.

EUGENIA

Move-out. No...well, at least not...didn't you read what it—

COURTENAY

You showed me—last week, the notice from the management company.

EUGENIA

No-no-no. Where's what I put on your door? Let me show you, it—

COURTENAY

'Gen...

EUGENIA

I sent out notices all right, but I didn't send out *their* notices.

COURTENAY

What are you talkin' about?

EUGENIA

If you'd take two seconds of your sweet time and just read it over. Where ya got it?

COURTENAY
(Looking around, not remembering.)

I got it...I got it put up here, woman...somewhere.

EUGENIA

It's *my* words...not theirs. Personal memo from *me*. It's not that little thing I showed you before.

COURTENAY

What are you doing, 'gen?

EUGENIA

You find it, you look at it. It tells everybody what's up, what the property company and the investors are trying to just slide on by. I called the Housing Authority, Court. I been running things on the up and up for too long 'round here just to—

COURTENAY

What's happening?

EUGENIA

What's happening is my big news. What's happening is that I'm not gonna let them do just whatever it is that they want to do, at least not without—

COURTENAY

But you said...

EUGENIA

I said, I said. I said a lot. I got caught up in thinkin' too much 'bout my own self. If I'd been thinkin' about all the tenants—*my* tenants, I'm the one who takes care of things around here, not them—

COURTENAY

'Gen, you know what you're doin' here?

EUGENIA

I know exactly what I'm doin' here. And truth be told, the day I walked in here and told you 'bout my meetin' with the little lady and her sketches, I knew exactly what to do then, too. But I let myself go and get nervous, worryin' about *me* too much. Then I remembered—I got *outta* my head long enough to remember—I got a responsibility to the folks here. I've *always* put people first--before anything else. People and what they need, *first*. Why go changin' now?

COURTENAY

These investors...like you said, they can make things happen. In Miami, money talks the talk.

EUGENIA

Yeah. Money talks the talk—talks the talk everywhere, all right. But you know what I finally decided? Sometimes you just gotta tell money to shut the hell up. What the company's doin', what the investors want, it's illegal and they know it is. I suppose they just wanna see what all they can get by with. But I'm not gonna be a part of it. I got the number of the Housing Authority on those notices, that notice you got put down *somewhere,* and I'm askin' everyone in the building to give a call to—

COURTENAY
(Coming to life, pleased.)
You are outta control, woman. You're all over the place. You're takin' care of business.

EUGENIA
Umh-hmm. Takin' care of business. We got a right, everybody here's got a right *to due process* no matter what plans they got for this building.

COURTENAY
But how much longer you think this *due process* is gonna give everybody?

EUGENIA
Well...I imagine once everything is said and done, everyone'll have 'til 'bout the end of February. Somethin' like that. Not much--but a helluva a lot better than Happy New Year, now kiss your ass goodbye. If they're gonna do a sweep of this place, they're gonna do it right. So you go right ahead and settle back now and *enjoy* your Christmas—like we all got the right to...*like we all got the right to.*
(Shakes her head, angry. Sighs, lets it go.)
And you keep somethin' in the forefront of your mind, hear? You got five good shopping days left to buy me somethin' nice.

COURTENAY
You're quite a woman, 'gen.

EUGENIA
Ohhhh...don't go embarrassin' me. Just do this woman a favor, could ya? I'm askin' everyone in the building to call up the Housing Authority themselves. I've filed a complaint, but it'd sure get some real attention if *everybody* here—

COURTENAY
I getcha, I gotcha. But you know, the management company and the rest of 'em, they're gonna wanna have words with you when they catch up to what's happening here.

EUGENIA
Ohhhhh, I bet they'll have *all kinds* of words with me. And for me. And about me. But I'm pretty good at comin' up with words, too. I bet I can be—
(Amused at herself.)

EUGENIA cont'd

They thought the riots were bad—*wellllll*, I tell you, once I get started...I can show 'em a thing or two, don't worry yourself.

COURTENAY

Am I lookin' worried here?

EUGENIA

I plan on landin' on my feet, Court. What else?
                (She smiles at him, and he returns the smile...but there is something
                about her demeanor that seems strained—as if beneath all the resolve, she
                is still apprehensive.)
Just burns me up—the lack of simple respect that they...that's what it is. That all it comes down to—a lack of—

COURTENAY

Uhm-hmm, simple respect. Simple respect for—respectin' people's privacy? People's personal possessions?

EUGENIA

Ohhhhh, nowwww.

COURTENAY

Uhm-hmm.

EUGENIA

And everything was goin' so nice. Oh, Court—you know I didn't mean anything about you comin' here...you know.

COURTENAY

Maybe. But I just like to feel that, 'til they set me outta here on my heels, that I got *some* kinda something here—my space—least for now.

EUGENIA

I know...it's just...it's hard...knowing just how to deal with...*concern*. Being somebody's landlady and somebody's—friend. I mean, if I'm speakin' outta turn here, you just let me know. I've always had trouble knowing if somebody's really a friend, really likes bein' 'round and listenin' to me, or if I've just talked 'em down into a coma.

COURTENAY

We're friends, 'gen. We're friends just fine.

EUGENIA

                (Delighted, but trying not to appear overly enthusiastic.)
I'm mean, I was just wonderin'. I just like to—

COURTENAY

We're friends just fine. But still, *friends* don't usually come in and start diggin' around in people's stuff. I don't take to my stuff bein' dug around in.

EUGENIA

I know. I just...

(Straightforward, without excuses.)

I'm sorry.

(He gives a slight nod.)

But it was nice comin' in and seein' that you got that trunk open. And if you don't mind, I got one question, *one* question I just gotta ask—and then I swear, I'll shut up. One question, I swear.

(COURTENAY simply looks at her. EUGENIA refers to the trunk's contents.)

Was she the grand love of your life?

COURTENAY

(After a beat.)

She should have been.

(There is pause as COURTENAY stares at the keepsakes.)

EUGENIA

(Quietly.)

I'll leave you alone to reminisce, Mr. Dees. But you think about givin' a call and filin' with Housing Authority, now. Ring 'em up. Just gotta let 'em know that people aren't to be *abused*.

COURTENAY

(Eyes still on the keepsakes.)

Cheated.

EUGENIA

(Heading to the door.)

We all gotta respect each other. That's the rule. If we can just remember that, then we'll get through. Remind me of that if I go and forget it again.

COURTENAY

(He breaks his stare from the keepsake items and looks at EUGENIA.)

I'll remind you of that if you go and forget it again.

(EUGENIA exits. COURTENAY turns away and looks into the room, drawn back to the keepsake items. He begins to move toward the trunk, and reaches for the old vanity record with trepidation. After picking up the record, he pauses and then moves to the kitchen. He places the record on a countertop, then digs through a cabinet of kitchen items to find the phone book. He thumbs through it and appears to find the information he is looking for. He dials the phone. As he holds the receiver between his shoulder and neck, he holds the record in his hands—studying it as if it somehow will reveal something to him. On the phone:)

COURTENAY cont'd

Yes, I'm looking to report a—I mean, to file a complaint. I'm a tenant, I rent an apartment in—to hold? Hold for what? Fine, fine—I guess so.

(He is put on hold; exasperatedly.)

My God, *God bless.*

(He stays on the line, becoming slowly lost in memory. Lights fade to black.)

ACT II
scene iv

(Lighting within the 1948 area rises slowly and is dim and "otherworldly." It is night. A projection, used as a backdrop, reflects an image of the New Orleans' French Quarter near Bourbon and Bienville. The sound of sensual, improvised jazz is heard at a low volume. Y. JACK is seen drunk and clinging, in his numbed condition, to a streetlight. As he mumbles to himself, the jazz fades.)

Y. JACK

We can...I know somebody...

(At first, LOLA RAE is just on the periphery of the acting area. The scene that will transpire between Y. JACK and LOLA RAE is part drunken blur for Y. JACK, part memory, part very real—and completely painful for both individuals.)

LOLA RAE

Oh, Jack...I can't believe...

(LOLA RAE begins to enter the acting area.)

Y. JACK

What are you doin'? What're you thinkin' you can follow...you knew exactly what you—

LOLA RAE

Jack...

Y. JACK

Like a puppy dog.

LOLA RAE

I don't want to remember you like...

Y. JACK

If it was another time and I...*but I can't.*

LOLA RAE

Jack, I—

Y. JACK

Who told you I was here?

LOLA RAE

You told me before, you said—

Y. JACK

I can't help you the way you'd like me to, the way you'd really—

LOLA RAE

I don't know what to do, who can I go to but you? Who can—

Y. JACK

I know somebody. If we...we'll get you to Kansas City, this doctor I know can take care of this, and then you and your—

LOLA RAE

What...

Y. JACK

Nobody'll ever hafta to know, just—

LOLA RAE

What are you saying?

Y. JACK

It's the only way I know, Lola Rae...I got a life to live...I got—

LOLA RAE
(Completely broken.)

What are you saying?

Y. JACK

You want my help, this is the help I can give you.

LOLA RAE

No, this isn't—

Y. JACK

You can't expect nothin' else—

LOLA RAE

This is not how I want to remember us.

Y. JACK
(Growing violent, losing his balance, lost.)

This is all I can—you can't expect nothin' else from me! You get away from me with all that.
(LOLA RAE moves out of memory, out of the acting area. Y. JACK
grows quiet.)
You get away from me. You get away…

(Y. COURTENAY approaches, and the scene takes on less of a surreal quality, and more of a stark/sobering aesthetic.)

Y. COURTENAY

C'mon, Jack. Let me help ya back to where you're stayin'.

Y. JACK

What?

Y. COURTENAY

We've both had enough for tonight.

Y. JACK

Hotel.

Y. COURTENAY

Looks like you had enough for just about everybody. C'mon.

Y. JACK

I can't go back to the Monteleone...Tiny's not covering me no more.

Y. COURTENAY

Tiny's not covered any of the guys at the Monteleone since the gig last month. Things've been hard since the bookin' at the Biltmore got cancelled. Set Tiny—set us *all*—way back. C'mon now, let me help ya. Y'hang out here like this, a cop's gonna come for you.

Y. JACK

So you guys got another gig lined up yet? Or you just hanging out and gettin' hungry?

Y. COURTENAY

I told ya before, Tiny's takin' the band to Chicago in a couple of weeks. The guys just gotta ride out the lean spell and then--

Y. JACK

Soooo, you gonna be playing the Aragon, or the Trianon, or the Panther Room? I guess all of you think you're some kinda big shots, goddamn big shots. Well, you can have Tiny Stevens. If startin' my own band bothers him so much...it's not like it's any skin off his ass.

Y. COURTENAY

You know it's not ya wantin' your band, it's... you know he told ya to walk 'cause he can't take a whole lotta what you like to dish out to him—in front of the other guys, and comin' in to rehearse when you please.

Y. JACK

He's nothin' but a goddamn...
    (Y. JACK falls on his face.)

Y. COURTENAY

You okay there, man?

Y. JACK

What the hell do you care if I'm okay? We coulda made somethin', Court.

Y. COURTENAY

I keep tellin' ya, Jack. I'd like to keep what we got goin'—*as I can*...as we can get together. I just can't walk with you. I owe it to Jewel to--

Y. JACK

You think that interests me?

Y. COURTENAY

Listen...I think the song's got somethin'. Maybe could be another *Confessin'* or *String of Pearls*. Who knows?

Y. JACK

Don't go doin' me any favors, Mr. Hit Parade. The song...what do you care about the song? If you cared somethin' about the song, you woulda walked out on Tiny after he let me go...you're just some Uncle Tom.

Y. COURTENAY

Your liquor's talkin'.

Y. JACK

I'm talkin'. And if you can't stomach it then move on. Just move on from the bastard with no gig, no prospects, no you. 'Cause ya know what? I don't *need* anybody, I don't need nothin', I don't need no one. I especially don't need you—why'd I ever bother with you?

Y. COURTENAY

Just point me in the direction of where you're stayin' and—

Y. JACK

It started up 'bout six months ago—Tiny's havin' trouble gettin' gigs on top of each other. Tryin' to hawk the big ol' sound. You know what the real trouble is? We were, all of us, born just a little too late. People are sayin' it...Big Band's startin' to dry up...it's just gonna get worse. Even if Tiny crawled to me now and begged me to stay, even if you and I made somethin' outta the song...we were born too late. That big ol' sound...we're just ridin' on its coattails.

Y. COURTENAY

You need yourself a bed, Jack.

Y. JACK

No job...no prospects...no money. Some girl whinin' and cryin' 'bout somethin' she brought on herself. It's too much. And it's all hooked up into the music, what I wanted to fill me up, but instead just...makes me feel more empty. Why do you think that is, Court?

Y. COURTENAY

I don't know, Jack.

Y. JACK

I think you do. I think you know it all and you're just not sharin'.

Y COURTENAY

I really don't know nothin', Jack. I just play. I breathe and I play.

Y. JACK

Well, I guess you got the world by its ear.

Y. COURTENAY

Am I leavin' you here? You really want me to just leave you here?

Y. JACK

I guess if I had the kinda sound you got I wouldn't waste it on some bastard like me. You're right—I shoulda kissed Tiny's ass—

Y. COURTENAY

I never said you should—

Y. JACK

I shoulda sent Lola Rae home that night. I shoulda sent that little girl home. I shoulda done...a lotta things in my life...that'd keep these great big empty feelin's away. I thought the music could...it's all I got, it's all I got to—

Y. COURTENAY

It's all any of us got, Jack.

Y. JACK
(After a beat.)
No...no, you got it. I don't really got nothin'...nothin' but baggage.

Y. COURTENAY

You're gonna go on. There's life after Tiny Stevens and God knows...you don't need me.

Y. JACK

You just wanted the gig, huh? Never really interested in...

Y. COURTENAY

I just don't see how—if there was *somehow*, Jack—but I just can't see how I can make it fit, *right now*. I gotta do right by Jewel, and with Tiny—

Y. JACK

Tiny—you think you got such a sweet deal with Tiny—you don't make even half of what—

Y. COURTENAY

I know how things are, *still*—

Y. JACK

You think he cares somethin' about you?

Y. COURTENAY

I don't care what he thinks of me, or if he cares about me, that's not what—

Y. JACK

He wasn't interested in anything about you 'til he realized he could get outta payin' a full salary takin' you on. You see, Court, y'see...there's musician's salary, and then—I bet you didn't know this, I bet you didn't know—there's musician's salary, and then there's nigger's salary.

Y. COURTENAY
(After a beat.)

Ya said too much, Jack—I don't care if you're—you've gone and said too much now. You have gone—
(Y. COURTENAY begins to lose his control.)
—and said w*ay too much.* Way, way*, way...*
(Y. COURTENAY turns to leave.)

Y. JACK

Hey! Hey, don't you turn your back on me. Don't you turn your back on me, *boy.*

Y. COURTENAY
(In a cold and almost frightening tone.)

Just leave me alone.

Y. JACK

Do what? You tellin' me what to do now?
(Y. JACK shoves Y. COURTENAY.)
Huh? You tellin' me what to do, boy?
(Y. JACK shoves again.)
You throwin' the orders around here?
(Grabs Y. COURTENAY by the collar.)
Huh?

Y. COURTENAY

Get your hands off.

Y. JACK
(Takes a jab at Y. COURTENAY.)
You throwing the orders around here?

Y. COURTENAY

Oh—nowwww.

Y. JACK

Huh? You feelin' like you're the boss?
> (Punches Y. COURTENAY.)

Feelin' like you're the boss man, huh? Come on...
> (Punches Y. COURTENAY again. As Y. JACK takes another swing, Y. COURTENAY defends himself. Y. JACK, in his drunken state, is no real match for Y. COURTENAY. After a struggle and one good swing from Y. COURTENAY, Y. JACK ends up on the ground.)

Y. COURTENAY

So this is how you want it. Well, Jack—you got it. *You got it*, just how you want it, it's all yours.

Y. JACK

Screw you.

Y. COURTENAY

Your mess. I don't want it, none of it.
> (Y. COURTENAY begins to leave again. As he turns, Y. JACK jumps up onto Y. COURTENAY's back. Y. JACK brings Y. COURTENAY to the ground. In the struggle, Y. JACK ends up on top of Y. COURTENAY; Y. JACK takes out/opens a butterfly knife.)

Y. COURTENAY

Jack...

Y. JACK

Got your attention, huh?

Y. COURTENAY

Jack...oh, God—Jack...

Y. JACK

A real attention getter, a real headliner, huh?
> (Puts the knife up to Y. COURTENAY's throat.)

Y. COURTENAY

Oh, God—Jack, no...no, please God, no...

> (Y. JACK suddenly takes the knife away from Y. COURTENAY's throat, grabs Y. COURTENAY's wrist, and forces the knife into Y. COURTENAY's hand. Y. JACK forcibly grips Y. COURTENAY's hand around the knife and does not let go.)

Y. JACK

Here. Do yourself a favor, y'do everyone a favor—go right ahead, take me outta everybody's misery. Ya go right ahead...

Y. COURTENAY

Let go, this ain't—

Y. JACK

Do *me* the favor. Ya want to.

Y. COURTENAY

I ain't doin' nothin'.

(Y. COURTENAY struggles to get away, trying to throw Y. JACK off of him. Y. JACK's grip on the knife and Y. COURTENAY's hand remain as they struggle.)

Y. JACK

You owe me somethin', you know you owe me somethin'.

Y. COURTENAY

Goddamn it, Jack—let go—get—

Y. JACK

You owe me somethin'—you wouldn't be so high and mighty if I'd never...do me the favor...go on—do me the favor...

(In the struggle, Y. JACK, forcing Y. COURTENAY's hand, receives a stab in the abdomen. Y. JACK screams in pain, as Y. COURTENAY finally breaks away/leaps away from Y. JACK.)

Y. COURTENAY

(Scared, on the verge of crazed tears.)

Oh, God—Jack. No...oh, God, goddamn it, Jack.

Y. JACK

(Holding his abdomen, in terrible pain.)

Now you can go. *I* say. *Now* you go. Better get your ass—

Y. COURTENAY

Oh, Jack. Oh, God.

Y. JACK

'Cause if anybody finds you 'round here...'cause if...ohhhhhh...

Y. COURTENAY

(Not knowing what to do.)

God.

Y. JACK

You don't want nobody to find you 'round here. Better get just as far away as...'cause if they....
(Moves his hand to reveal blood.)
ohhhhhh...
(Y. COURTENAY leans in slightly to Y. JACK.)
You better just—*ohhhhhh.*
(Y. JACK slumps in pain.)

Y. COURTENAY

Jack...oh, Jack.

(Y. COURTENAY takes a final look at Y. JACK, then quickly looks around and finds a direction in which to run. After Y. COURTENAY clears the area completely, Y. JACK peers up. He starts to reach for the knife which has ended up a few feet away from him. As he takes the knife in hand, he suddenly slumps over in agony, and holds his abdomen. He drops the knife, and begins to emit an awful, sad, choked sob, riddled with gutteral sounds. He raises his head and his eyes are seen—wild, filled with tears. He sobs louder, clutching his bleeding abdomen, consciousness flickering away. Blackout.)

ACT II
scene v

(Lights up. COURTENAY's Miami Beach apartment, late 1988. It is night. The apartment is illumed by a streetlight shining into the kitchen window. The sofa is opened to reveal bedding, tossed about by a restless sleeper. COURTENAY sits on the floor near the trunk; he wears pajama bottoms and an old t-shirt. He holds the small, slightly yellowed wedding dress in his arms. JEWEL, seen at the same age, in the same costume as in I-x, sits on the kitchen table staring at COURTENAY. He holds the dress up before him, and then embraces it as if JEWEL is in the dress. JEWEL, still seated on the table, reaches out to him. When he releases the embrace and begins to slowly fold the dress into a manageable bundle, JEWEL slowly drops her arms. He puts the dress into the trunk and then begins to put the other keepsakes slowly back into the trunk. Last of all, COURTENAY reaches for the vanity record and stares at it for a moment. A very light knock is heard at the door. JEWEL begins to cross out of the apartment. He sets the record aside and goes to the door. As he cautiously answers the door, JEWEL exits out of his apartment proper, disappearing past the fringes of the set and sightlines, staring back at him all the way—until the exit is complete.

As COURTENAY opens the door, JACK is seen; he wears a bright, short sleeve shirt. There is silence between the two men for a moment, then JACK speaks.)

JACK

I couldn't sleep.

COURTENAY

Sundries shop on the corner, 24 hour. They got Sleep-Eeze.

JACK

I couldn't sleep good for about ten years after that night, Court. Even now, I still have dreams.

COURTENAY

So now—you come to say your piece? Or we gonna talk about your condo some more?

JACK

Can I...may I come in?

> (COURTENAY opens the door wide for JACK. As JACK enters, COURTENAY turns on a single light, leaving the room still slightly in shadow.)

COURTENAY

Sorry 'bout the sofa bein' spread open, I don't do much entertainin' at 4am.

JACK

If I don't say what I need to say—right now—I'm afraid it's all gonna slip from me. I'm sorry for the hour, I...

COURTENAY

I don't sleep so good either, Jack. The hour's no real concern—just talk.

JACK

I still see her eyes...her deep brown—almost jet...her eyes. And I think to myself...what kind of idiot, *cruel* idiot, was I to say the things I said to her? I keep coming back to her. The music's in there, yes, and a lotta other things—but even after all these years, it's her I keep comin' back to. And it makes me crazy 'cause Lola Rae was one girl out of a *hundred* I've known. Guys back when I played, they had a new girl—maybe two—in every town. So why do I...after all this time...

COURTENAY

We all have different lessons to learn. Maybe she's just tied up with somethin' you never reckoned with. Maybe she *wasn't* just one gal out of a hundred.

JACK

I wonder what I'd do if I could just go back and...

COURTENAY

And what, Jack?

JACK

Do whatever it was I shoulda done. I've carried a lot of empty feelin's around with me, Court. And I've had my time to think about this and I want to say—to you...I've never been too good at handling...I don't know...neediness. Seems strange that the things people have trouble handlin' end up doggin' 'em the most. I've spent my life trying to understand so much.

COURTENAY

Unfinished business.

JACK

When I think back, there's a point in time—right when everybody I knew went away to fight—that I think things inside of me started to get real hungry. When I was kid, and all the guys I knew

JACK cont'd

were goin' off to be a part of the war, I stayed behind. I worked on the railroad to support my
mother, never had any kinda father other than my Granddad.

COURTENAY

Sounds like a sob story, Jack.

JACK

I know. But even so, I was a young man tryin' to find some kinda place in the world and I
couldn't get around the fact that I was startin' out with this empty feelin' inside...tryin' to make
a buncha dream fill me up inside... and angry at anything or anybody that I felt got in the way of
that. Never stopping to think that maybe my "salvation" was gonna come from my *realities*,
people and things that were real and tangible. I just kept tryin' to deal in dreams.

COURTENAY

If you think you're tellin' me somethin' I don't already know—about your emptiness and such—
I know, Jack. I knew. Maybe that's why I took so much off you, more than a reasonable person
would or should. I thought that maybe whatever you were missin', *maybe* somethin' would come
along and—

JACK

And she did. I had so many answers to so many questions that I was askin' myself—right in that
little girl. I had the chance to be what I wanted, to be some kinda somebody...it was all right
there in her eyes. But instead of realizing that, I felt like she was in the way. I was so sure the
music was where I was gonna find the answers. Too much dealing in dreams.

COURTENAY

So now 40 years later you look me up just to tell me 'bout the one that got away.

JACK

I'm just tryin' to tell ya—now bear with me—

COURTENAY

I'm here.

JACK

About the *music*...it wasn't ever the music's place to make me whole. I shoulda been married to
Lola Rae, 'cause I'd always been lookin' for somethin' precious *and there she was*. I shoulda
been a Daddy, 'cause I never had one. And I shoulda been a *friend* to you, not whatever the hell it
was I ended up bein' to you. Those were my realities. And truth be told, they had all the music in
'em that I needed. I got lost in the music of the Big Band, 'stead of dealing with the music of my
own life. For me, music was just s'pose to underscore life's lessons, wasn't meant to open up any
secrets of the universe for me. Maybe Benny Goodman or Artie Shaw held some secrets when
they played, but for me...I needed to be dealin' in realities.

COURTENAY

The past is just what it is, can't revamp now. Your life—the life you got now—sounds pretty sweet to me. You got your fine condo in Pompano.

JACK

To hide away in...my 950 square feet away from the world, hidin' away from who I shoulda been.
(Pause.)
I am sorry for who I was. And because of that, in many ways, I'm sorry for who I am now. I'm sorry that—

COURTENAY

I don't need to hear nothin' more about you bein' sorry.

JACK

I tried to fill up the emptiness inside of me by tearin' you apart.

COURTENAY

You give yourself too much credit. If there was anyone who tore me apart, it wasn't you.

JACK

(Frustrated.)
I don't know what else to say, I'm trying to...I'm trying to say—

COURTENAY

You've said a whole lot.

JACK

I'm trying to—I want to tell you—our music...*what we had was good*—

COURTENAY

It was damn good.

JACK

It was goddamn good. But I took it and I used it in a way that—

COURTENAY

Jack—Jack, man—you've said plenty now. Maybe you should just sit back and listen a little bit instead.

JACK

Listen?
(Sighs, calms himself.)
Oh, hell. You're right...I'm sure you got a lot to unload, too. I bet you got some *choice* words for me, I'm sure. Choice ones.

COURTENAY

No. I don't. I...whenever I've thought about the *possibility* you and I might ever see each other again, I've thought very little 'bout what kinda *words* we'd say. You've brought a lotta words here with you tonight, you're saying a lotta big things here, but the truth is...I don't have any words for you. In my head, it was *words* that were ugly between us.

>   (Pause, as the two men truly connect.)

You gonna bring me my horn?

>   (After a moment, JACK looks around and spots COURTENAY's horn
>   case. JACK picks it up slowly, opens it, and takes the trombone from the
>   case. He carries the horn to COURTENAY and puts it down before him.
>   He stands frozen before COURTENAY as tears spill down over his
>   cheeks.)

ACT II
scene vi

(Lights up. COURTENAY's Miami Beach apartment, late 1988. It is the morning of the next day. Street sounds of South Beach, the radio, and the bathroom shower are heard. COURTENAY is seen in trousers, but still wears the old t-shirt he wore in the earlier scene. He is at the stove making scrambled eggs as a pot of coffee brews on the kitchen counter. The sofabed is now closed. The trunk remains open, with the vanity record nearby.)

RADIO BROADCASTER 1
(A male voice with Cuban/Spanish dialect traces.)
…into the village of Lockerbie, Scotland. Further information on the crash of this London to New York, Pan Am flight will be made available as it released.
(A few tones of the station's transition music are heard.)
The holiday traffic report is sponsored by Velvet Creme Donuts...live traffic reports from--
(COURTENAY's phone rings.)
--in and around the major malls in Dade and Broward counties.
(COURTENAY turns off the radio, takes the eggs off of the stove, and answers the phone.)

COURTENAY
Hello? Mornin', 'gen. No, I'm up. Makin' a breakfast for a houseguest. *He*...he's just in town for...no, he's got a room at The Fontainebleau, it's just-uh, last night we reminisced here 'stead of sleepin'. Yeah—I did, *I did*. Uh-huh. You're kiddin'. Well, isn't that somethin', 'gen, that is truly...*you* are remarkable. So we got till when, now? March. Uhmmm—well, better than a kick in the head.
(Sounds of the shower stop.)
Hey—I think I better be—*what?* Sure, if I'm not around, let 'em in—but keep an eye on 'em. I'll be out for a while, got work lined up this mornin' in Miami Shores, gonna play holiday tunes. Uhm-hmm. Say, when ya let the exterminator people in, *you* feel free to come on in, too. There'll be somethin' for you on the kitchen table you can save up for Christmas mornin'.
(JACK enters from the bathroom area, wearing trousers, towel drying his hair. His dress shirt is slung over a shoulder. A deep, jagged scar on his stomach is clearly seen.)
I should be goin' now. Uhm-hmm. But ya give me a call later 'bout your gift. Ya let me know how it suits you.
(COURTENAY sees the scar as JACK puts on his shirt.)

JACK
Thanks for lettin' me use the facilities. The shower in my *fine* room at The Fontainebleau alternates between scalding and freezing. More excitement than I can handle. Makin' eggs?

COURTENAY

It's what I got. You want a plate?

JACK

(As he puts on his shoes.)

Nahhh, can't. I'm a cholesterol making machine.

COURTENAY

I see.

JACK

Y'know...it's been good—it was good of ya to play and...catch me up on you. I hope that you're not gonna be missin' your sleep later on.

COURTENAY

Awww...I woulda probably been up all night anyway.

(Putting the eggs onto a plate.)

So you're drivin' to Texas.

JACK

I'm drivin' to Texas.

COURTENAY

(Eating.)

Gonna see him.

JACK

Gonna see him and his family.

COURTENAY

That's nice, Jack—I mean that. That's a good thing to have now, it bein' the holidays and all.

JACK

Well, I think it *may* be. I don't know what he's really expectin', or what I should say. I wonder about exactly what she told him. Seems like I have somethin' to live up to, but it just...aw, the whole thing just astonishes me.

COURTENAY

Astonishin' that a son wants to look at his father?

JACK

Not that...that *she*...that *Lola Rae*...

(Pause, then JACK simply sighs, shakes his head and moves on.)

I wanted to ask you...

COURTENAY

You ask me.

JACK

You...how much longer were you with Tiny after...you know—*after...*

COURTENAY

I got the hell out of the Quarter—out of New Orleans—out of Louisiana—*right* after.

JACK

Yeah. I guess that you-uh...

COURTENAY

Uhm-hmm.

JACK

Yeah.

COURTENAY

(After a beat.)
Since things are bein' asked, I wanted ask you...

JACK

Ask.

COURTENAY

How come you...what kept you from taking your last good breath out there on Bienville?

JACK

Cop picked me up. Took me to the county hospital, didn't even ask me for any kinda story. Called me a shitfaced drunk and stuck me with a ticket for vagrancy.

COURTENAY

You were in pretty bad shape?

JACK

I lived. Lived to traipse on around the country for a while more, tryin' to put work together, never really knowin' my place. Then the be-boppers started to come in. That was sunset. Couldn't stand it, couldn't stand a lotta things, got out. How'd you keep afloat?

COURTENAY

I just play, Jack. I never needed the Big Band, never needed any kind of band. Workin' with Tiny, a gig like that—that kinda money was somethin' I thought I needed, but when it was over, I never missed it. In fact, bein' free to play when and where I wanted—I was glad to have that back again.

JACK

I thought the money was somethin' you needed to do right by Jewel.

COURTENAY

I never did do right by Jewel—money or none. I shoulda...

COURTENAY cont'd
(Spies the vanity record.)
You know what...you should...
(Gets the record.)
Here, you take this. Give this to...give this to William. This is something he should have.

JACK
What...
(Realizes.)
The song.

COURTENAY
Yeah. He should have this. It's pretty much his legacy. This...
(Somewhere in his own head as he speaks, realizing.)
All these years...and the music's been...
(Referring to the record.)
Right here...never left.
(Touches his own chest, his heart.)
And right here...never left. The music holds its own. Doesn't need nobody or nothin'. We shouldn't, we don't need...
(Looking at the opened trunk.)
I never needed to make sure that the music's taken care of. We're who need taking care of, not the music.

JACK
Sounds like you got religion.

COURTENAY
You know, Jack...you and I mighta had a lotta differences...but when it all comes right down to it, we've both been guilty of the same damned thing.

JACK
What does it all come down to?

COURTENAY
Like you said--the dealin' in dreams. Thinking that taking care of business is the only business, thinking that breathin' and playin' is the same thing. You know, I have this—this friend around here. And she says—well, she says a *lot*—but she mentioned something about people that I wish I coulda understood about million years ago. Something I wish I understood back when I left my own realities standin' there, time after time, with this sad smile on her face that seemed to say—go on and deal in dreams, but don't forget the way home.

JACK
Your Jewel.

COURTENAY
Shoulda been dealing in people before dealing in dreams.

JACK

You really think you could have?

COURTENAY

I *should* have...but I never really believed that the music would still be waitin' for me at the end of the day. I left *her* to wait and gave myself away over and over to the sound and the thrill. Gave myself away too easy. Not ever able to just *sit still* for even a second and maybe give life the chance to unfold around me. Always chasin' and movin'. Givin' myself away to the some*thing* that I love, but not to the some*one*.

JACK
(With irony.)

Not that I ever had the guts to admit it, but I always thought *you* were the one who saw things straight.

COURTENAY

Wasn't able to see at all, Jack.

JACK

You had your own baggage.

COURTENAY
(Turning to the trunk.)

Uhm-hmmm...and I been haulin' it around with me for a little bit a'forever.

JACK
(Pause. JACK nods then looks back at the old 78 he holds in his hands.)

You think he can find something that'd play this?

COURTENAY
(Turning away from the trunk.)

If he found *you*, I'm sure he can find something to spin a 78.

JACK

You sure you wanna...

COURTENAY

It's his, Jack.

(JACK accepts the 78 silently. He clutches it more closely than he consciously realizes as the following dialogue transpires.)

JACK

Well, I guess this is...about it.

COURTENAY

I guess so.

JACK

Yeah.

COURTENAY

Yeah.

JACK

Maybe I'll ring ya again sometime.

COURTENAY

Maybe.

JACK

I'll keep your number and address handy. Who knows, we might...

COURTENAY

Who knows?

JACK

Sure.

(JACK finishes buttoning his shirt.)

COURTENAY

Cuttin' over to Miami Shores today. Got a gig.
(Picks up his wristwatch off the kitchen table and checks the time.)
Just lemme grab a shirt, and I'll head out with ya. I gotta make a bus.
(Goes to grab a shirt from the closet.)

JACK

I gotta be makin' tracks, too. Why don't I just meet ya downstairs on the street and...

COURTENAY

(Putting the dress shirt on over his t-shirt, buttoning up.)
That's fine.

JACK

And then we'll move on.
(JACK goes to the door but pauses before he lets himself out. He looks
at the record, turns back to COURTENAY and smiles, then exits.
COURTENAY tucks in his shirt, puts his trombone in its case and grabs
his wallet and keys. He pauses, looks at the trunk, then looks
out and around the apartment.)

COURTENAY

I'm just sorry, Jewel. Sorry that I'm such a slow learner, baby.

(He kneels before the trunk, straightens the keepsakes, then reaches to close the lid. His arm and hand freeze before he can grasp the lid, then they begin to tremble. He pauses and waits for the tremor to pass. It subsides and he grasps the lid and slowly closes the trunk. He blinks and realizes that his eyes have welled over with tears. He wipes the tears away in astonishment. He smiles. More tears flow as he looks out and around the apartment. He rubs the tears away, trying to catch them on his fingertips. He finds his bandana and carefully wipes his eyes. He then rises and gets his Panama hat, drops his bandana inside of it, and puts the hat on. He starts to pick up his trombone case but then stops. He crosses to the kitchen and reaches on top of the refrigerator for the Publix grocery sack. He opens it and removes an *enormous* can of Folger's coffee and a stick-on Christmas ribbon. He puts the ribbon on the can, and places the can on the kitchen table. He gives a quick nod, pleased. COURTENAY then picks up his trombone case, goes to the door, looks back at the closed trunk a final time, and exits.)

The End